Mind

Beyond

Matter

The Mandela Effect

Dedications

This book is dedicated to all those who have been affected by the phenomenon known as the Mandela Effect.

I would like to send out a special thanks to all of my Mandela Effected Family, especially John Ross (photohelix)

Written by Anthony Santosusso
Edited by Susso & Jade Smith
Cover Design and Chapter Art by John Ross
Published By A&A Publishing 2018

Table of Contents

IN THE BEGINNING ...

I find myself wanting to discover and write something that will help people understand what is really going on in the world today. Something that will open the hearts of people who are locked in the system, who do nothing but work and sleep, work and sleep and stay asleep. I feel as though I owe it to my friends, not just those I have met throughout my life, but the friends who I have confided in even without meeting in the flesh, a true account from my Spirit, of the events that occurred in my life that woke me up to the truth, or what isn't the truth.

No matter how I justify that introduction, it is nothing more than my ego. Pure ego. If I were a complete enlightened being, then I would finish this book right here. For that matter, it would never have been written or even the thought of it entertained. But, I am not a fully complete enlightened being in this Timeline ... what was that? ... this Timeline? ...

What I feel I can do, is portray specific accounts that took place in my life that woke me up or lifted the veil. I can describe, from my own involvement, the phenomenon known as the Mandela Effect and give you my interpretations of the many supernatural experiences I have had over the past few years. By doing this, I teach myself and maybe even reach people who have had one or more of these experiences, letting them see, that they are not alone.

So, what is the Mandela Effect? The Mainstream media will try to convince you that it is a number of people misremembering things. And since that is the first place most people go for answers, it gets blown off as another lunatic conspiracy. Trolls (those who know everything) will debunk everything including the idea that one person can have a Mandela Effect experience. Why is that? Is there an agenda there? In simple terms, the Mandela Effect is when one or more people recall a past event, pop culture, or a product differently than it presently is. And it is not that these things have changed, because it seems these things have always been the way they are currently portrayed. How can thousands of people have the same wrong memory, at the same time in history? When you come to the realization that it is a real phenomenon or when you have a memory that doesn't fit, you start to question physical reality, your reality, and then life, and then death …

Yes, I know, so many questions. Is the Mandela Effect a natural occurrence and we have only just now noticed it because of computers and other technology? Is there a higher power involved? Is someone or something doing this on purpose? If so, who is doing it and why? Is this how we naturally evolve? What are the catalysts to seeing changes? Is a traumatic event or even death a catalyst? Are we on another Earth or in another realm or universe? Or are we in a transition? Is it all just a computer simulation? I do not know. Yet, I do have theories and hypotheses based on firsthand experience. For me, the Mandela Effects are simply signposts, a signal that your consciousness has shifted into another Dimension, Density or Timeline. Truly, for most people, the Mandela Effect is not that simple or easy to wrap your head around. What I didn't understand when my journey began, was how someone could see a change that is impossible and blow it off and justify it as if everything was normal. Well, I couldn't understand then, but I do now, because I realize I did it all the time, over the years. And you probably have as well.

After three years of immersion with significant material, I have come to the idea that there is, more than likely, something complex coming our way, that will wake even the most stubborn soul. Those who have witnessed Mandela Effects and other strange events over the past few years will be called to help those who are fearful and confused over whatever the future holds. The thing is, it might not be as obvious as people noticing changes in history.

Along with the experiences and my interpretations, I also carry the weight of knowing that I do not truly know what the Mandela Effect is or why it is happening. Mainly because, more than likely, there is more than one cause, person, place or thing involved. From the experiences I will be sharing, I have come to feel that we are multidimensional beings experiencing multiple timelines and it is natural. But, we could also be experiencing physical reality through a computer program. Or life may actually be linear and somehow things may actually be changing. Or it could be a combination of those and other theories. But I don't feel that these things are changing. I feel that it is you that changes.

As much as I would love to give you all of the answers, all I have are some of my answers. And that is what I intend to leave here, my experiences along with the answers and questions I surmised. If I come across as if I know what is going on, it is only my experience talking with passion and a love for the truth.

The truth is, I believe that I will always be on a search, because what I have found, is that truths and beliefs shift and change. Yes, beliefs are your truth and because they are merely beliefs, they can change. There can be multiple truths and the only one that matters, is the one you focus on or the one you are conscious of. On top of that, no one can tell you what that truth is. That, is up to you to find.

Although, I do write quite often, mainly poems and metaphysical explorations, this will be my first published work. Forgive me, as the path I took for writing this information was how it all happened chronologically, yet each time I wrote about a subject, it would remind me of something else, because it is all connected. So, the foundation of this information is in chronological order, yet at times it seems I am all over the place. I do believe you will enjoy it, all the same.

The information contained in this book comes from multiple supernatural paranormal experiences and the interpretations that came from those experiences.

MIND BEYOND MATTER

Perception is the key to transforming your reality. What you focus on is your perception, which shows you your reality. Consciousness is the conduit to your perception and your reality. You are energy and energy cannot be created or destroyed. You know, I never understood that last statement and always took it as science fact. This way I really didn't have to understand it. It is science, after all. Your perception of reality is just that, yours. And the feelings and emotions you attain and release from your heart, play a large part in what you will experience through your perception. Understanding where you are, in relation to who and what you really are, is also key. I may have a good idea about some things, but the truth is that there are so many factors involved, that I would be hard pressed to believe that there is only one answer for anything you are about to read.

If you can recognize your perception, and focus your vibration and the energy you are putting out into the world, then you can influence your consciousness and shift your consciousness to a reality more to your liking. Is it that simple? Sounds like looking into a Ma*gic mirror on the Wall* and having your questions answered. What if physical reality is both subjective and malleable? What if, it is just that simple? Feel it, know it and create it. What I have experienced and what I am about to explain is much more than just a game. Yet, I can't help to examine the possibility of life being just that, a game. If I didn't, then I wouldn't be open to all possibilities. And that is something I must be. If I may describe life as a game, then we are the players and the multidimensional realm is the playing field. Where did that come from? That comes from over two years of powerful, unexplainable, bizarre, paranormal experiences. And it wasn't just the experiences themselves. These events brought up more questions and the answers were coming in by means of the supernatural. And after all of the experiences I have had and all of the information I have gathered and explored, with all of the research and experimenting, one thing stuck in my mind that intrigued me. It is not the answer by any means, but would shed much light on many things. What are we, as intrigued human beings, really looking for? What would give us our answers? We really want to know who we really are. We want to know what it means to not be physical, assuming we are much more than just flesh and bone. If we had the answer to that question alone, people and events would be much different. As this may be a true statement, it may also be part of the process of our growth. Even if this wasn't the plan, it is the plan now. This is part of the lesson we need to understand. Experiencing physical reality seems to be much more than what we have experienced in the last two thousand plus years. It seems our knowledge has been stifled. Yes, the argument could be made that we did this to ourselves, we put ourselves to sleep, and we probably did, but now it is time to wake up.

The list of strange experiences that all came knocking at my door started with the 'Mandela Effect'. It was the Mandela Effect that was the one paranormal supernatural experience that I had, that went commercial. I will state now, that in my opinion, the title Mandela Effect does not tell the whole story and is not a proper term for this phenomenon. It is no one's fault. When the Mandela Effect first hit the internet, no one had theories as to why this phenomenon was occurring and as far as anyone knew, it was the only circumstance, of that type, that anyone was aware of. Actually, that is not true. There have been people experiencing this phenomenon and describing it with other titles. There have recently been reports of people recalling past events that could be labeled a Mandela

Effect, myself included. Now, over the past two years, the Mandela Effect has grown so much so, that there are theories on top of theories spreading themselves all over the internet. I will state it here and repeat it again. It is advised to discern everything you read for yourself. Feel with your heart, what is right for you before blindly believing anything you are told by anyone, including myself. So again, what is the Mandela Effect?

Starting from the beginning and in its simplest form, the Mandela Effect got its name because many people, myself included, recall Nelson Mandela dying in the late eighties or early nineties, only to discover that he became the President of South Africa, sometime after his death. I recall watching the funeral on television because I have a trigger point.

I worked at Trump Plaza Casino Hotel in Atlantic City for many years. It was a day like any other when I walked into the break room and saw a good friend of mine, who would be my roommate in Mississippi some twenty years later, sitting watching a funeral. I asked him who died. He said, Nelson Mandela. I watched the screen and I saw Bill and *Hillary* Clinton walking around shaking hands and such. My friend is African American and is very much into his culture. I didn't want to ask, but I did anyway. "So, who is Nelson Mandela?" I got such a punch in the arm, that I would remember who Nelson Mandela was for the rest of my life. This is my trigger point. I have a memorable experience with finding out who Nelson Mandela was and what he has done in his life. So, I know he died, right? No, I just know I saw his funeral and apparently he died again. Understand that the idea that something you know to be true, never being true in the first place, will get some heads scratching.

The fairest way I can define the Mandela Effect, would be people noticing changes in history that cannot be explained. From experience, I can honestly tell you that it is not misremembering or confabulation. That doesn't mean there cannot be people out there misremembering events and song lyrics. Although, I have a personal list of Mandela Effects that I am one hundred percent sure are not the way they were in my past, there are several Mandela Effects that I am not sure of, except that things look different or off. I suggest following your heart. I recommend watching videos on YouTube about the Mandela Effect and if you are so inclined to read everything you can on the subject, but know that your answers will come from within, not from another's experiences, videos or writings.

When I first started experiencing these strange events, I was excited to be sure, but I was also pretty shaken up. It has been three years since I was conscious of my first experience. I was not always this confident and secure with what seems to be going on. One theory is that we are experiencing physical reality in a computer program; that can't be easy to grasp. And if it is only our consciousness that is experiencing things and that is why things are changing, well it is going to take some time to get used to that as well. It took months, maybe a year for me to straighten up and be composed. This is a serious topic. Although, what I have seen, is people tend to get complacent. Once you become content, the game is over. I am not saying, if you are affected by the Mandela Effect that you should stop making jokes and stop having a good time. No, it's the Mandela Effects that put life back into my soul. What I am saying is that there is a time and place for everything. Since physical reality is different from what tens of thousands of people remember, it seems to me that something serious is happening. I'm saying it's time to buckle your seatbelts. It is going to be a very interesting ride, and we should be prepared for anything. But, how would one prepare for a change in history? And what does it mean if our history is changing?

I would suggest knowing that physical reality is not what you have been told. I surmised this by several means, one of which was surfing YouTube for answers. I also started doing my own videos. I did not jump on YouTube making videos like it was my job. I only got onto YouTube after much deliberation with myself. I decided to start doing videos because I felt they might reach and help others, and I also quickly realized I was teaching myself.

So, how does someone come to terms with being lied to about major information and move on? From the day you were born you have been programmed by your parents, your teachers, friends, family and peers, even if unknowingly by them. Interacting with these people and society as a whole is what created your personality. So, who are you really? How did you come to believe the things you believe now? And why is it that we all seemed to easily accept everything that we have been told without question? How come we accepted what has been told to us by authority and not question it? For me it was about finding the right question. How could I completely accept the idea of an infinite universe, but could not accept the idea of our blue marble being more like an infinite plain? Why couldn't I accept it or even explore it and truthfully, what does it matter? I have my answer, and optimistically maybe it can help guide you to find your answers.

YOUTH AND SPIRIT

It seems that my whole life has been set up for this exact moment in time. It seems that for my whole life I have been on a never-ending search for the truth. But, the truth of what? Since the early eighties, I have been interested in and have examined just about every conspiracy theory or mystery that had surfaced. Unidentified flying objects, area 51, the Bermuda triangle, GMO's, the Loch Ness Monster, cloning, ghosts, bigfoot, mysterious disappearances, time travel, pyramids and yes, even all kinds of aliens and their underground bases. I studied most religions. I was on the fence with everything, even if I denied it to myself. I say that, because I always leaned towards believing in most of these things, even if I didn't have an experience with them, which would make these things truth. And that in itself isn't very shrewd of me. Just because one believes something, doesn't mean it is real or true. It is the experience that makes something real to an individual. For the past two years it has come to my attention that facts, truth and beliefs change. How can something be a fact, if it changes? Having an experience is more knowing than listening to others' facts or opinions. Listening to others' accounts, including mine, does not make it a fact. It does for the person having the experience, but to others, it is only a fascinating or enlightening story that may spark a future experience for the person listening, or help them in some other way. But it is still not fact. The thing is, having an experience is not something we can presently command to happen. All we can do is explore other people's accounts of events, until we are blessed with an experience, and when that does happen, your perception of the reality you live in will change greatly.

I was always exploring and listening to others' accounts of events, hoping one day I might have an experience. I did, and I have grown more in tune with the more recent personal experiences and forgot all about my childhood experiences. Looking back on my life, I did have paranormal events happen as a young child.

When I was very young, I had several experiences where I was speaking with something or someone. I have no recollection to what the conversations were about, I just feel like they were always around if I needed them. I felt safe with them around. Most of what I remember is seeing one single, bright, tiny, spark of a light, but my feelings were that it was a group of Beings. And now, that is how I am comfortable speaking about them.

When I was about four or five years old, I had an experience that I can recall quite clearly, even though others in my family seem to vaguely recall the incident and some don't recall it at all. You will have to finish the book to understand the significance of that statement. I was in the front yard by myself and I distinctively remember that I was playing Cowboys and Indians, until I heard the police siren and I quickly change the game to cops and robbers. This simple change in games seems to be a trigger point for me. That simple change made it a significant part of my life worth remembering.

The sirens were becoming louder, and I felt an urge to look up. I looked up and saw the familiar, bright gleaming spark of a light hovering over my head. It conveyed to me that it also wanted to play and suggested that we hide from the bad guys behind my father's red *Volkswagen Beetle*. I immediately agreed and ran behind the car. The light then conveyed to me, firmly, yet pleasant at the same time, to hide behind the wheel of the car and to stay out of sight. I immediately did as it asked. After a minute or so I looked up at it and explained to it that I wanted to see what was going on. The light was deliberate yet calm when they answered in the negative. I really wanted to see what was going on but I knew not to disobey my friends, the spark of light. The sirens became so loud that I knew they had to be close. I looked back up at this light, which to me seemed like a perfectly normal thing to do. I was not afraid by any means and I knew I had to listen to its direction. It wasn't overpowering me. It let me make my discussions, but its suggestions would have been just as obvious as if the directions were coming from a parent. I mean, there were police cars chasing someone near my home and I felt safe hiding with this spark of light. I asked them once again if I could see what was going on and they replied that I could, but only when they said that I could. I was very excited. I asked, "Now?" Not yet, was the reply. I waited a bit and again I asked and they said yes. I threw my head around the wheel of the car and I saw a tall man running in-between my house and the neighbor's house. They, or rather it called me back behind the wheel of the car. I sat up, just staring at the light. They told me they were leaving and I should stay right where I was until my mother came outside. I agreed and they vanished.

When my mother came out from the house, I ran from behind the car and jumped into her arms. She held me tight and approached a police officer getting out of his car, as a number of other police cars started pulling up in front of my house. I don't recall the conversation itself, just bits and pieces. All I kept doing was pointing where the man ran. Eventually a couple of officers took my advice and ran between the houses. I don't know how much time had passed, but at some point I heard my mother talking with someone on the telephone saying that the officer told her that they knew this man and that he was very dangerous and so desperate, that if I was seen by him, he would have grabbed me and took me with him as a hostage.

When I was about ten or eleven, I really believed I could be a decent poet and artist. I wrote some pretty advanced stuff for a young boy that age. When I wrote I felt inspired and I would imagine my spiritual friends guiding me to write the words. For many years I carried five copybooks around filled with poems. Sadly, I haven't been able to locate them and they are not around today.

One of the more artistic things I did was draw many cartoonish make-believe characters, one on each page of a copybook. I remember spending a lot of time on these pictures. Some were animal like and others were machine like. And I always imagined them interacting with each other. Some fifteen plus years later, I was in a toy store staring at one of the animal like creatures I drew back then. My mind was disordered. I was confused and didn't understand how it was possible. I wouldn't have been interested in it at all, but the one drawing was extremely accurate, no it was exactly what I drew. I mean scary exact. Amazingly, I also initially blew it off and bought these things called *Pokémon Cards* for my daughter. As time went by, I started to take a closer look at these *Pokémon Cards*. I didn't really know what to think. I recalled some of the pictures being similar to the one hundred plus pictures I drew over fifteen years earlier, but there was no way to be sure. I wasn't really that taken by the situation and just blew it off.

As soon as time allowed, I travelled over to my mother's house and dug up all of the old books I wrote and drew in. This is when I took the five copybooks for prosperity. Unfortunately, the book with the drawings of the characters I drew, were nowhere to be found.

The group of what may have been spiritual beings left me around the age of twelve. Or maybe society got too close and I had to imagine them away. Either way they showed up again at about the age of nineteen when I was seriously questioning my catholic upbringing. I got down on my hands and knees, pounding the floor and screamed at the air telling Jesus I wanted the answer! I demanded an answer! The light was not as brilliant as when I was a child and I feel it may not have been physically there at all, when it told me very insistently that I was to research and do the work for myself. And ever since that day I have been on a search for the truth.

THE AWAKENING

Ever since I can remember, I was never concerned with what others would think about my ideas, my projects, my abilities, my companions, my jobs and anything else that would be listed under the category of what I felt was necessary for me to express my life. Quite simply and forcefully, because it is my life! So, where do I begin this lengthy chapter of my life that must be documented? I could start at the beginning of my strange involvements, except for the fact that there were paranormal and supernatural experiences going on, at this particular time in my life, before I was aware that there was even a definition for such things. At least, for the things I was experiencing. It seems these experiences would be better placed as flash-backs for the reader to better understand the meaning behind each of those specific experiences. If I were to start from the beginning I would be writing about how I always had my nose in some conspiracy and that, at this specific time, around late 2014, there was nothing to be found. At least, that I hadn't already explored, before my eyes were truly opened in early 2015. I was tired of searching and even when I did, I was always coming up with nothing. I have studied unidentified flying objects my whole life and never actually seen one. Oh, I looked up into the night sky enough times to say I saw some light move from here to there and then disappear and granted they were unidentified, but to have seen an actual flying disk? No, I can't say I have.

The boredom of not researching paranormal experiences was bugging me. Sure, I was distracting myself with movies, social media and other computer outlets, but this was becoming more and more mundane by the day. There had to be something new to discover. I started with weather patterns and ended up with volcanoes. I watched Yosemite volcano videos on YouTube for over a week, as they spoke of one going off any day in February of 2015. I was content with the volcano information, so I pushed on. Every once in a while, my eye would catch an EMP fear mongering video or something even more strange on the suggestion side of the YouTube page. I ignored those feeds for as long as I could. I kept coming across some nonsense about Mother Earth being flat. My thoughts at the time were something along the lines of, oh my, how are people aloud to record and post such rubbish? The significance of watching the volcano videos will be better understood after other events and personal experiences are explained. At that time, I did not realize that watching volcano videos would actually have some part of a future theory based on some of the dealings I was experiencing. It was the experiences that I have had since 2015, that blew my mind or more correctly, seriously lifted the veil.

At that time, I was being exposed to these paranormal, supernatural experiences, and I didn't know it. The one phenomenon that took place with me that also went commercial, hitting the Internet on YouTube, Reddit and other media outlets, was The Mandela Effect. Please understand, that there are many theories as to what it is and what is causing it. And if you do any engine search, most of the first twenty or so suggestions will steer you in the direction that the Mandela Effect is just a bunch of people misremembering stuff. They blow it off as some crackpot conspiracy. Yet, with the experiences that took place in my life, I can say for certain that it is not some conspiracy. It is a real thing and I have hypothesized on a few theories. As for having a straight forward answer, my suggestion would be to steer clear of anyone claiming to know exactly what the Mandela Effect is. I only say this because there are so many things taking place at this time in 'this' history and so many of the theories could be placed inside one another, that it is too complex to say one way or another. Suffice it to say, that there are many people who claim history is different than they recall. People are noticing changes with geography, products and pop-culture. And it is not the idea that these things are changing that is the freaky part, it is that these things have always been the way they are now.

Because of the experiences I have had, and what it seems may be taking place, by my definition, it is my opinion, that it is absolutely possible for one person to experience a Mandela Effect. This is derived from the idea that there are infinite timelines. But, I am repeating myself and getting ahead of myself. Okay, take a breath. For a few months, I had the unnerving experience of being the only person who remembered the Big Dipper and Little Dipper being connected. It took almost a half of a year for someone to confirm my memory by having that same memory about the Dippers. Of course that was with the help of my YouTube channel. Yet, personal Mandela Effects are few and far between. Only because they are not normally recognized. How many times would you say you blew something off because it made no sense at all? Have you ever misplaced your keys, knowing for sure where you placed them? Most people aren't mentally prepared to come out and start telling everyone they noticed changes in history that cannot be explained. And rightly so, as any authority figure would recommend medication.

Time Travel, Merging Earths and Shifting Consciousness are just but a few, of the more known theories. Because of my many experiences, I have theorized that we are the Dimensional Beings we have been looking for. To be more precise, we are Multidimensional Beings and our Dominate Consciousness is Shifting through Infinite Timelines, and that it is more than likely our Natural State of Being. So, when people notice lyrics in an old song have changed or a product that is spelled differently than they recall, all they are seeing is what it has always been, in that particular Timeline. Nothing is changing! Nothing has changed, except for you! Seeing a Mandela Effect becomes nothing more than a signal, message or signpost that your Consciousness has shifted into another adjacent Timeline. I would hypothesize that the greater or more obvious the 'change' is would mean there was a bigger gap in-between said Timelines.

Dominate Consciousness? It seems to be a term I have coined, meaning where your present consciousness resides. If the theory stands correct or even close to correct, than there are many adjacent Timelines branching off every nano-second or at the very least, every time a human-being makes a decision or choice. Your physical body interacts with other people on every Timeline that you exist in. But, where you are conscious, is where your Dominate Consciousness resides, as the others will only become apparent if you happen to Shift into one of those other Timelines. It may even be that these said Timelines only exist when they are needed, called upon or in use. When I say, "Dominate Consciousness", I mean, where you're Conscious is, in relation to all of the other Timelines. You may exist in all or just some Timelines, but where you are Focused and Conscious, is your Dominate Consciousness. Your Dominate Consciousness is all you ever need to concern yourself with. I also feel, that it is very plausible, that we will eventually be Dominantly Conscious in more than one Timeline and be able to consciously go back and forth through Time. Although, this idea would be advanced, the reason for it may help other areas of interest. One reason I feel we may be able to exist in more than one Timeline, comes from people having dual memories. For instance, some people have reported recalling two distinctly different events taking place in their life, when only one of those memories is possible. A little less intense experience might be noticing words in a song changed. *The Beatles* comes to mind. The first line in the song, *'With a Little Help from My Friends'*, states, *"What would you do/think, if I sang out of tune"?* Some people recall both 'do' and 'think'. I have been writing a documentary since 2001, about the mystery surrounding the life and death of *Paul McCartney*. This documentary theorizes that Paul died long before the myth suggests. To purposely digress, I halted the *Paul McCartney* project after experiencing the Mandela Effect, especially with people coming back from the dead. It seemed to me it was going to be a lot easier to replace Paul knowing how to Shift in and out of other Timelines. I went to this document for reference as soon as I heard about this possible Beatles Mandela Effect. The information itself was placed on a USB chip in June of 2015, just before my computer crashed. As a matter of fact, the computer crashed and I did not have the information saved. At this time I had nothing backed-up. I did everything I could to get that computer running again. After about five minutes, I got it started with no screen. Then, for no reason, somehow, some way, the screen came up and I had complete access for about two minutes, and that's all I needed. The information was saved and the computer was trashed. The information stored on the USB chip had the word, 'Think' not 'Do. This is what is considered a dual memory. As much time as I've spent listening to the Beatles, I am surprised that I don't have a definite answer for this one, but I feel when someone is close to a Mandela Effect topic, they themselves do not see the change. I sing 'think', but everyone I ask to sing or say the first line of, *'With A Little Help from My Friends'*, they reply, *'What would you Do…"* Infinite Timelines and Infinite Dimensions make this very possible. This dual memory idea comes out clear when asking someone what color the Yield sign is. Well, over eighty-five percent of the people asked, answer 'yellow' and are sure and then some people get that look on their face and with a question in their answer they reply, wait red? Back in 2017 when I looked this up, I discovered that the Yield sign hasn't been Yellow since 1972 and that that information has changed a couple of times since, as well. Also, many people remember both *Berenstain* and Berenstein. Some people remember *Jif* and *Jiffy* on the shelves at the same time, Myself being one of them, while others are sure *Jiffy* turned into *Jif* and some even say it used to be spelled *Jiff*. Some people recall *Curious George* having a tail with others saying he never had a tail. Infinite Timelines, maybe? If true, then the idea that there are infinite Timelines becomes a very conceivable option. And wherever you are conscious and focused is where your Dominate Consciousness resides. Now let's be sensible. All we should ever be concerned with is where we are conscious, right? Now consider the idea that you can shift your Dominate Consciousness wherever you like.

The idea about being able to go back and forth through time by means of our Dominate Consciousness, stems from a few of the experiences that took place, mainly when I moved to Mississippi. After moving back to Colorado there was one event that took place that struck me as a possible time phenomenon. I was enjoying a day in the Hot Springs when myself and another gentleman I just met, named Mark, started conversing. He had a medium length white beard and looked as though he was very healthy for being in his early seventies. When I felt that the time was right, I started with the Mandela Effect questions. He had a look on his face I hadn't ever seen while asking these questions. Than he seemed to get serious. He just listened as I went on about some of the other, noncommercial, experiences I had. I mentioned death being a possible catalyst for seeing the Mandela Effects. It went on for a good half an hour until he started to vacate the pool, and as an afterthought, asking me my last name. I told him and then explained that Susso was my YouTube channel and that it was part of my last name. Then something came over me. I felt as though I should ask him what his last name was, so I did. Not a word was spoken after he answered me. I stared at him and he starred back with a very slight grin on his face, one of knowing. He simply stated for me to keep doing what I was doing and that his last name was Twain.

Now, when I said that Shifting our Consciousness through Timelines may be our Natural State of Being, what I mean to say is, that every nano-second we are Shifting into another directly adjacent Timeline. This is how we create motion and time. Each Timeline consists of multiple parallel realities within that specific Timeline's parameters. I am speculating that most of the time we stay within our foremost Timeline, or at least, we used to. When we notice a change that cannot be explained, we have Jumped to an adjacent Timeline consisting of different parameters.

Although, I feel that Shifting Timelines is our natural way of existing, it has been suggested that these Shifts are being purposefully done on a mass scale. What I like to call a "Forced Mass Shift". But who is doing it and why? Well, 'CERN' has come up and the 'D-Wave Computer'. Some say the Illuminati or the Governments that control the world. Some say it's the devil and others say it's God. Why? It's really anyone's guess. Nefarious reasons, evolutionary reasons, maybe to keep control or maybe it's just natural. These questions become obsolete when you start to realize you can manipulate or use this information to Shift your Consciousness into a Timeline, more to your liking. But again, I am getting way ahead of myself. I also feel there could be what might be referred to as a "Natural Mass Shift". This would be explained as a natural disaster, or some climatic tragedy that caused many deaths. Like a volcano eruption, maybe?

Please understand, this is all theory but more accurately these are my hypotheses based on the experiences that took place in my life. Not just the experiences by themselves, but also the way I interpreted those experiences. So, it is also important to understand that these experiences were for me and that someone else may have interpreted the experiences differently. Hypothesis, Theory and Speculation, can all be true, from **_your_** perspective. These are my truths and my beliefs, which constantly shift and change. If it were not for these events that took place in my life, I would not understand that truth and beliefs change. This is not something that came to me in a dream, or that I meditated on or something I picked up, off of other people. The Mandela

Effect is most definitely real to me. It is just one of the many supernatural events that took place in my life, starting in 2015 that had me looking at the world differently. Yet, it was not the Mandela Effect alone, which changed my perception of reality. It was going to take a greater event to convince me that 'everything' we have been taught is and has been a lie. Even though, that may only be the case on these relevant Timelines.

As far as a long look at my background, for this presentation, all you really need to know is that I was always on the lookout for the unknown or esoteric. I studied everything from different religions to government conspiracies. In the nineteen eighties and through the nineteen nineties, I worked in a casino in Atlantic City, where myself and four others would sit and discuss all kinds of conspiracies. We delved into esoteric information and supposedly top secret information, with material from people like, Vladimir Valerian and his book, '*Matrix II*', or William Cooper's, '*Behold A Pale Horse*'. We always talked about how physical reality was not real. How our real selves were in Spirit. It did not take long for me to latch on to the idea that death, was one of the biggest illusions. We don't die! Of course, I assumed we would shed the Physical body and move on to a lighter, less dense body. Why, do I say, 'assumed'? To be honest, when I started to feel that death was not real, I didn't mean it literally. I didn't mean that the body I resided in would go on forever. I felt that I would always know myself, as I am, on some level, although that idea has been ripped away. On one specific memorable day, in the spring of 2015, my ideas, perception and thoughts about death, seriously changed.

THE IMPALEMENT

      It was deep in the month of May, a brisk, dark morning in 2015. The night before I had cleaned my bedroom, utterly spotless. I may have some form of Obsessive-Compulsive Disorder, as sometimes I feel as though whatever project I am working on, must be finished and completed in perfect fashion. It was that urge that innocently filled my body that morning. So, when I woke up and noticed a small piece of paper on the floor, damn if I was going to throw it out in the clean trash can. I crawled out of bed. Barely able to open my eyes, I grabbed my robe and threw it on. Being too tired to bother with tying the tassel, I bent over and grabbed the piece of paper, and made my way to the door. I laughed to myself, realizing I was headed out of the back of the house and through the garage to put this small piece of paper in the garbage can out on the street. It was still dark out, for the most part. It was about 5am, and just a small amount of light was peering through the dew covered morning trees. I reached the garage door, glancing over at the football sized quartz, I had sitting in the backyard. My first impression, as I opened the door, was that it was too dark to jet across the garage floor. Yet, I could see the light at the bottom of the door at the other end of the garage. Keeping my eye on the light at the bottom of the door, I felt I could make the casual stroll to the other side of the garage. So, I shut the door and didn't bother flicking the light on that was merely two inches from my hand.

I do not believe I finished my first step, when the adventure began. As I took that first and only step, one of the tassels from my robe became tangled around a shovel that was stretched out in front of me, which I had propped up along the garage wall, the night before. The other tassel became twisted around my left knee, keeping that knee from bending. My other knee completely locked, having my right foot awkwardly tucked under the shovel. My right hand was in the pocket of my robe, desperately trying to escape and my left hand was selfishly clinging onto the piece of scrap paper, which looking back, become the main catalyst in this unnerving experience.

My entire body was as stiff as a board and there was nothing I could do, but wait for the impact. I fell straight down like a heavy weight. It was immediate and quick. I hit the edge of a very sharp glass table stored on its side. Would you believe, that I was the one who put the table there, the day before, mumbling to myself that I should move it behind the larger rounded edge thick wood table, because someone could really get hurt? Synchronicity, at its finest.

The next thing I remember, was my jaw hitting the ground. I have no or little memory of anything penetrating my body. Whatever took place, between the time the left side of my chest impacted the sharp table edge and my jaw hitting the cement floor, is unknown to me. It was like it all happened in a split second. It was almost like I skipped that part. Also understand, that the edge of the table was just over two feet off the ground. My chest hit the edge of the table and my jaw hit the cement floor. How was that possible? I couldn't see a thing as it was still very dark, and that bothered me because something didn't feel right, and I could not see. I was in a very awkward position on all fours and slowly tried to move. That 'something' that did not feel right was really making me nervous. I felt something trying to push its way out through my back. This sensation happened a few times before I realized something penetrated me. I recall being very confused and wondering what I should do. And again, something did not feel right. It was not the feeling of pain so much, but more of an uncomfortable knowing. I did assume my body was going to hurt something fierce, and that it just didn't register in my brain yet. It also occurred to me that there was going to be some blood. I wasn't sure how much, until I started to push myself up. Immediately, I thought, 'oh shit, this is going to hurt badly and there is going to be a lot more than just some blood'. I froze for maybe a good minute before I decided to throw myself off of the table and run for a phone. I say good minute, but honestly, with this whole event, time was still. I started to push myself up and I could feel the table coming out of me. But, it didn't hurt. There was no pain. I was expecting blood to start gushing everywhere and I was preparing myself to stay focused, thinking I may lose consciousness. I finished pulling myself from the table and grabbed my chest with both hands. I stood up and reluctantly taking one hand from my chest, I reached for the light switch, flicking it up. The room became extremely bright by the artificial light blinding me from being able to search for my injuries. Everything just froze, almost like I was in the middle of a meditation. I just stared. After what seemed like forever, I slowly moved my hands and took many glances at my tee-shirt expecting to see red, but saw nothing. I tried to pull my shirt down. I couldn't. I was more emotional trying to rip my tee-shirt off than when the impalement took place. I finally was able to rip the tee-shirt. I was expecting a major gash. There was nothing. I stood in shock, looking around the room. There was no sign of blood, which would have been the most obvious difference. I immediately noticed that the table that I felt leaving my body, was now behind the large rounded wood table, where I had intended on putting it. I did not move it, nor did my roommates, as I questioned them thoroughly the next day. The entire week ahead, my body was in much pain. Not my chest, but my back. Normally, I would blow that off as the L-5 problem I had, or that pain that would shoot up my right leg, but that was now on the left. They both seemed to disappear completely, after about a week.

Now, you understand what I meant when I stated, that I felt death was an illusion, that it wasn't real, and that when I first came to the idea about the death lie in the 1980's, that I didn't mean it literally. But, that seems to be the case with this experience. Yet, with these experiences and my analytical mind, I feel that my consciousness just shifted from one Timeline consisting of specific parameters to another Timeline with slightly different parameters. But to be quite honest, it could be something so much more. It could be something I just can't understand … yet.

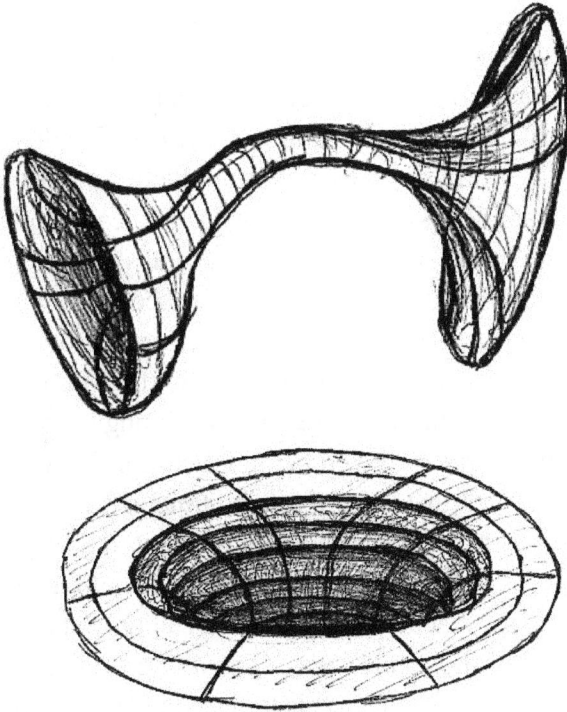

QUANTUM IMMORTALITY

Now, this 'we don't die' idea brings me back to when I first started driving back in the early eighties. It was dusk and I was driving on I-95 in Philadelphia PA, with the rain hitting my windshield to a point where I was barely able to see. There was an eighteen-wheeler on my right and another one on my left; both trucks were just about three or four car lengths in front of me. As a teenager, I am not really sure what was going through my head, I just knew I wanted to get away from these trucks. So, I hit the gas to shoot between them. I realized instantly that I had lost control of the car. The driver side wheels took flight. The car was on the two passenger side wheels and I was up off the ground. There were many things going on in my head at this point. Total shock being one. The experience lasted no more than three seconds. One second I was in the air and the next I was back on all four tires, still behind the trucks. With my heart pounding a million miles a second, and with my entire body stiffening up, I slowed the car down and stayed well behind them for the rest of the trip. Did you catch that? There was no time in between when the car was on two wheels and when it went to being on all four wheels. Thinking back on this now, I do not recall any impact from the car reaching the ground. I can only speculate that I was in total shock and I wasn't recalling everything properly.

Now, to connect this to the Mandela Effect. Shortly after this experience, I noticed McDonalds changed their sign. To me, it made it look more modern. Of course, I wouldn't have thought that they removed a letter, because the whole sign looked totally different to me. I do recall McDonalds being MacDonalds, but it didn't dawn on me until after being exposed to the Mandela Effect, three decades later. Why did I notice it at all? In theory. I may have died during the hydroplane experience and instead of passing on to the afterlife, my consciousness Shifted into another adjacent Timeline where I did not die, so that I may continue with my life.

So, this whole idea of Quantum Immortality, which there seems to be a plethora of information about on the internet, could be an actual way of life for us. Or maybe just some of us, depending on who and what is real. I do think this will all be connected to your own personal belief systems, as well. Your own personal experiences will be shown in a way you can understand it. You will only be shown what your mind can handle. If in actuality, I flipped that car back in the early eighties, anyone who was close to me, who may have focused on a strong fear of me dying, experienced me dying in that Timeline.

Another experience, which occurred close to New Year's Eve 2014, comes to mind. This event, coupled with other events in quick succession, could be why I started noticing different changes. I was alone in my apartment. My roommate was away for the holidays. I was in a rotten mood and I was looking for a good stiff drink. I opened the refrigerator door and saw a clear glass container with fruit in a clear liquid. Of course, I assumed it was vodka and drank most of it right down. It turns out that it was grain alcohol. The look in my eyes must have been horrifying. The realization of what I just swallowed, put me in a state of shock. I desperately reached for the kitchen sink, gasping for air that would not come. I turned the water on and grabbed as much water as I could, forcefully tossing it in my mouth. The sensation was very bland, and it felt like nothing was getting down my throat. I felt a tear roll down my cheek, which snapped my attention to the fact that I was slowly losing consciousness. I claimed one more handful of water before my knees hit the ground. I deliberately lied down on the kitchen floor hoping to catch a breath of air, but I blacked-out instead …

… I woke up on the bathroom floor, two rooms away with no recollection of how I got there. I still had a burning sensation in my throat, so I went right for the bathroom sink and drank more water. I walked around the apartment for a while feeling a bit buzzed, but not nearly as drunk as I should have been for the amount of grain alcohol I consumed.

After all of the experiences I have had since the impalement, I have come to hypothesize that our Consciousness Shifts into another similar, adjacent Timeline when death occurs. What I feel happens is your Consciousness locates, probably instantly, a parallel Timeline with similar parameters closest to the one you were just in. This may not be the case for everyone or every circumstance. It may be certain kinds of death, I do not know, but it seems that we continue on. For how long, would be another question I have not been able to answer, only speculate. Other experiences have shown me that it is just our Consciousness and not our bodies that Shift into other parallel Timelines. But this could just be for me and where I am in relation to my life, my beliefs, and my focus. Others may be having different experiences.

And please remember, that I do not have all the answers, if any. I am still searching and will search even if I think I have found the answer, because I know I have not. If someone believes they have the answer or an answer for the Mandela Effects or other phenomenon, be skeptical and question everything. Knowing anything for sure, is a trap. I may not have the answers you are looking for, but what I have, is my answers from my experience. You may have interpreted the experience similar to the way I interpreted them, or you may not have. You will need to do the work yourself. Since this term or theory of Quantum Immortality has been tossed around the internet, I have to say it would be one of the top theories that I resonate with.

ELVIS, JUPITER & PHO

It was sometime in early 2015, that I had an interesting experience, but I did not realize it. For that matter, everything was different for me, I just was not aware of what was happening. Or at least, I had no theories as to why I was noticing impossible changes and then justifying them away, by any means possible. As I have come to realize, most people do this without even realizing it and probably do it all the time. My roommates were just that way. They broke my balls at every turn. I mean it is true, everything does not have to be a Mandela Effect. Yet, if we Shift every nano-second, then in truth, everything is a Mandela Effect. But that may be a little deep and could get semantical. An important thing to know here is I was focused on Mandela Effects; my roommates were not.

One day, while walking into the living room, I noticed a commercial on the television about a movie called 'Jupiter Rising'. I recall this because one of my roommates mentioned that it looked like an interesting movie. At this time, I still believed in outer space and enjoyed science fiction. It could have been the next day, but more likely a week or two went by when I saw the same commercial, but the movie was called 'Jupiter Ascending'. Even though I was deep into studying the Mandela Effect, it did not hit me until months later, when it was pointed out on a website, that the title had changed. What? Why was that? Why did my mind instantly try to justify this misunderstanding in my head? Why wouldn't I have immediately thought it was a Mandela Effect? I would think I should have. But that was not the case. I just went about my business like I never saw it.

Is Elvis Presley still alive? This experience brings that whole idea back to life along with a twist with the Paul is Dead myth, but back to Elvis.

I was worked in a small casino in Colorado. On one particular day, I was dealing the game of craps. The game was dead, meaning it had no players, and a song came on that I never heard before and I thought it was pretty catchy. As I was listening, it occurred to me that the singer in the band sounded like he was trying to sound like Elvis Presley. Then I thought, no, he just sounds like an older, more mature version of Elvis. So, I say to one of the other dealers on the crap game, "Hey, this guy sounds a lot like Elvis." Well, one fellow employee thought that I was joking around as he started laughing while he spoke, saying something to the affect like, "You're kidding me, right? This is Elvis! This is one of his biggest hits!"

Now, I was sure this song was not one of Elvis Presley's biggest hits. It could have slipped by me, I suppose, but surely not a big hit. My father was a big Elvis Presley fan. Any time we talked about music, I spoke of the Beatles and he spoke of Elvis. I am quite sure I have heard everything Elvis did, even if I wasn't trying to. I even have some memories of watching a movie or at the very least walking by the television while one of his movies was on. To me, Elvis' biggest hits were Jailhouse Rock and Hound Dog. This song that was playing on the casino floor, was way too 'produced' to be an Elvis Presley song.

I looked at my fellow employee, thinking he was kidding, and I asked him what the name of the song was and when it came out. He responded with a statement that threw me for a loop. I do not recall the name of the song, because my brain was scrambling for answers. He said that this song was on his last album, and that it was released about a month before he died in 1977. Now, this I could not understand for sure. The whole idea of Elvis Presley dying in 1977 was extremely bizarre to me. It just was not possible. In the late 70's, probably 1979, I watched a documentary type movie on television about the life of Elvis Presley. I clearly recall the end of this show having words pass across the screen, filling in the end of his life. The information I took in as a fourteen-year-old boy, has always stuck in my head. What I read on the screen, was that Elvis had a heart attack on stage in Las Vegas and he was pulled backstage where he died, in 1972! I am absolutely sure that I have memories, not just of this television program, but of Elvis Presley dying in 1972. I never knew how he died, before watching this program. That is not something my father and I would have discussed. I feel that is why I had such a strong memory of this show and his death. Since this experience, I have spoken to others about these memories and after two years, only around five other people had also believed that Elvis Presley died in 1972.

I was affected by this thing called the Mandela Effect, yet I did not know it. I started to notice strange things. At the time, my mind was still justifying the Mandela Effects away. I was studying them, and I had been affected by them, but nothing was one hundred percent, as of yet. So, I would easily justify these changes away with misremembering something. The word *'confabulation'* has been kicked around the Mandela Effect community for over a year now, but at the time it had not surfaced yet.

As I was walking down a street one afternoon in a city just outside of Denver, Colorado, frantically looking for some place to eat, a large truck rolled by me. Looking up and making sure I was out of its path, I noticed that the *Pepsi* logo was different, I immediately assumed they changed their logo. I only found out later after getting back to my apartment, that the logo I was looking at had always been that way. For me, *Pepsi* had a thick wavy line on top and a thick wavy line on the bottom. Blue on top, red on the bottom with the word *Pepsi* written in script form, straight through the middle. When I searched for this old logo hoping for an answer, I did find one, but the words were printed, and the colors were the other way around. Red was on top and blue was on the bottom. On top of that it was a can from the early 1960's and it was for a diet *Pepsi*. It did not dawn on me until months later, but I am quite sure diet soda was not around until the seventies, with *Tab* being the first, coming to mind.

This same day I walked by, what I believed was a Chinese restaurant. It was called PHO and I was *definatley* pronouncing it wrong. (< yes, I know *'definitely'* is spelled wrong, but that is the way I was taught to spell it back in the seventies, in another Timeline). It turned out to be a restaurant featuring Chinese, Vietnamese, and Thai food. After talking with some of my friends, I was a bit embarrassed as they told me pho was bone soup and it has been around for quite some time. For me, it showed up in 2015.

I had another unknowing experience around this same time. My path to work was very routine and there was a convenient store that I frequently visited. Next to this store was another store that I never went into, but the sign always caught my attention because it was old, worn wood. It really needed a coat of paint badly. One day, I was driving by the stores and I noticed that the sign was new. It was plastic and it lit up. I thought nothing of it except that it was about time they changed their sign. The very next day the old, worn wood sign was back, like it was never replaced. I realize there are a few explanations for this, but with the weird things I had been noticing, why I would think anything except that it was probably one of those Mandela Effects.

I am going to skip ahead a bit with two experiences that are similar to the above experience. Granted, I was a little more familiar with the Mandela Effects as well as totally affected by them and I had quite a few different supernatural experiences by this time.

I had just moved into an area in the middle of the Colorado Rocky Mountains. A couple of miles from the apartment I was renting, was a convenient store. I took note of this store because it was the closest one, as the whole area can be somewhat remote. Once on the way home, I stopped in this store because I needed to use the restroom. I walked into this tiny room with one counter and a small man standing behind it. It was not a bright room and it was very musty and smelled of oil. I asked for the restroom and he pointed at a small door behind him. I thought this strange and thinking back it was like walking into a service station back in the seventies. I thanked him and left thinking nothing about it. Not a week went by as I stopped in this store again and it was completely modernized. It was much larger and was connected to a coffee shop and both stores shared these large bathrooms set in the back. It was not just the inside, but it was also the outside that was totally transformed with modern gas pumps with awnings, which is something I don't recall from my first visit.

Not long after that paranormal connection, I was heading into another store around the corner from my house. The sun was so bright I could barely open my eyes. I was standing in front of the door of the store when instead of going right in I decided to turn around to glance at the sun. I could not open my eyes at all and decided to just go into the store. I was no more than ten minutes in this store when I walked out the door and I could see fine. The sun was just as bright, but my eyes were shaded by the awning that was not there ten minutes prior. There is no way someone built an awning and ramp, no less, in ten minutes!

THE PITTSBURGH SHIFT

It could have been any night in late May or early June, when I started to become seriously aware of things being different. I saw changes yes, but even then, in early 2015, I was ignoring changes saying to myself that I couldn't prove it so it doesn't matter. But it was not just those visual changes. The air was different. Food tasted different. It was like I was living somewhere different, but everything was the same, save the Mandela Effect experiences. To be sure, I had no idea what was going on, so I was on alert and I was just keeping to myself, which was not in my character at all.

One windless June morning, I got home from work at about 3am, I turned on my computer first, as usual. Changed clothes and grabbed a beer. Everything was running like a well-oiled routine, until I looked at my YouTube feed. It was all Mandela Effect and Flat Earth material. Granted, at the time there were only maybe ten or fifteen Mandela Effect videos, but that topic seemed more fascinating to me than people believing the Earth was flat. The thing is, I was glancing at these Flat Earth videos on my feed since February 2015. Never actually clicked on one. I mean, come on, there was no way I was going to give these people an opportunity to waste my time, or was this me wasting my own time? I was more interested in the volcanos that could erupt at any moment. Then I see a video about the Berenstain Bears.

Here is where I must digress. Now, I recall seeing these bears, but the first time I saw them was probably late 2011, just after I moved to Pittsburgh PA. Maybe early 2012, but for the sake of argument I will date it sometime after September of 2011. For a reason I can only speculate on, I stared at these books for a good long minute, pondering the idea that there was a new children's book in publication. That is right! These bears never existed for me until 2011. So, it seems The Berenstain Bears have been around since 1962. I am not clear on how that could be possible as my daughter was reading everything under the sun for that age group and I would have read them to her as well. And there is a television cartoon show? No, it is not possible for me to have not known about these Berenstain Bears. I am absolutely sure I would have known about that these bears having been around since the sixties. I never watched them as a child for sure! And that is not even the discrepancy with the Berenstain Bears. The difference people see is the spelling. Many people, and I mean thousands, remember one hundred percent that the spelling was always *Berenstein Bears*. But, if you research these bears, you will find that the spelling is and always has been, *Berenstain Bears.*

What is even more interesting, is what happened the second day I lived in Pittsburgh prior to me noticing these bears. I was in a major car accident. I was on a major highway just outside of Pittsburgh, PA. I saw that the traffic up ahead was all stopped so I tried to get over into the next lane on the left. I could not even sneak through, I had to stay in the lane that was slowing by the second. I decided that I was in no rush and figured I would get off at the exit with the stopped traffic and get to know some of the area. All the traffic was stopped on the off ramp I was exiting. All but the eighteen-wheeler, which was three cars behind me. The first impact was familiar, being in a few fender benders, I recognized that sound of metal being crushed. My head was thrown into the steering wheel and it snapped back up. The second impact was the strongest, smashing out the back window of my car while simultaneously pushing my car under the SUV in front of me. My head was again thrown into the steering wheel and the airbag went off and popped. By the third and final impact, I just desperately wanted it to stop. I was pretty shaken up. I do not know how long I sat still in my car before I started slamming my body up against the door that just would not open. I gave it one hard push and it finally swung open. I tried getting out of the car three times before I realized I was being restrained by my seatbelt. I had to focus to get myself out of my car. I know I was in shock, so I just walked through some stunned people and sat on the side of the road waiting for assistance. The first car was cut in half and the driver died instantly. The second car, which was the car behind me was totaled and I heard that that occupant died days later. I was told that because the truck was empty, and my trunk was packed, that my life was spared. Any other scenario and I may have passed on.

But there is more. About twenty minutes before the accident, I was leaving the parking garage of the new job I just received. I sat and waited, taking in the moment. This was an exciting move for me. Philadelphia to Pittsburgh does not seem that great a distance after living across the country, but it was a big move for me at the time. At that time in my life, it was a custom or habit for me to rest my sunglasses on the 'V' of my neck. It is where my glasses hung while I sat in the parking garage, feeling renewed and trying to get through to a friend on my cell phone. I expected him to be right behind me, so I waited a good ten minutes and then decided to head out on my own. But before I left, I felt the most amazing feeling in my bones to remove the glasses from my neck. I immediately took them from my shirt collar and placed them on the passenger seat, where they would stay and be buried in a totaled car. Looking back, well there is no need to speculate on what may have been in other Timelines, far removed from the one I currently reside in, had I not removed those sunglasses.

To digress even further, not long after this accident, I had a dream. The dream itself may seem arbitrary but it is on point with the timing and my future experiences. It was not like any other normal dream I have ever had, rarely recalling dreams. When I do recall things while I sleep, they are much more than just dreams. There were three of 'me' in this dream. The 'me' I was Dominantly Conscious of was just listening and observing. The other two were deciding what path I would take from that point on. I do not remember the details, but I did feel I had a say and was involved. It went on for a while, but they did seem like they wanted to move along. Like, there were others as me that they had to figure out what to do with.

Anyway, back in 2015, the *Berenstain Bear* Mandela Effect did not pull me in. But I did not dismiss it, claiming these people were crazy and nuts and needed medication. Yes, you might be surprised at some of the comments you might get for speaking about your memories. How dare I remember things differently than you? I should be attacked! Can you feel the sarcasm?

I decided to look into the Mandela Effect further, wondering if there was anything I might recall differently. I did not want there to be, but when I saw a YouTube video by *Jesse Spots* on "*Sex and the City*" and "*Interview with the Vampire*", I knew, I was affected by the Mandela Effect. An ex-girlfriend had the "*Sex in the City*" VCR tapes. I may have bought a couple of them for her. And, I am quite sure I saw the movie "*Interview with a Vampire*", not '*the*' vampire. After seeing these videos and being sure that the present titles were not the way I remembered them, I called her up. Now, she is married with three children, so I was not sure how smoothly this conversation was going to go. Granted, she knew me well and knew I was into many different conspiracies while we were dating.

She most bizarre thing happened to me during this call. The conversation was seriously like a eulogy. I was a bit confused, but I was happy to hear her voice. She said things like, she is so grateful to have me in her life both then and now and that I would always be in her heart. After I listened to the pleasantries, I explained the reason for my call. She was intrigued by everything I said to her about some of the changes and I could hear questioning in her voice as I rattled off some of the more popular Mandela Effects of the time. After I questioned her for a good fifteen minutes, I asked her to get one of her old VCR tapes, if she still had them, of the show with the four girls that ran around New York City. She decided to humor me and grabbed one. She came back and read off, "*Sex **in** the City*". I paused a second and said, "Now, really look at the title on the box and read each word you see." And it happened. She started, "Sex …" I could hear that she was very confused and amazed at the same time. I asked her how sure she was that the television show was called, "*Sex **in** the City*" and she responded with absolutely one hundred percent. We talked some more as her mind was trying to gather that, if they changed the title of the television show, how could they have changed her VCR labels. Now something happened for the next month or so with my friend here. She was interested, and I kept her up to date with some changes by questioning her now and again. But she has a husband, three children, a job and I am sure pets as well. As I stated in one of my YouTube videos, which we will discuss the videos in a future chapter, some people just do not have time to be concerned with Shifting their Consciousness through Timelines. They have bills to pay and kids to feed. At this point, it has been over a year since I have spoken with her. Because of another experience I had with another family member, I am under the impression that she is not following the Mandela Effects or consciously Shifting Consciousness. She may have been, if I kept in touch, but as I like to say, her Dominate Consciousness is not riding along side of my Dominate Consciousness. To take that further without getting too far into 'New Age' philosophies, wherever your focus is, that is what you will experience. Try and understand that from my point of view, there have been a few things added to that way of thinking.

Another interesting experience is that I have gained memories from the parallel Timeline I jumped or shifted into. This brings us back to the, dual memories. One personal event for me, is remarkably interesting, but the details wain, so they will be excluded. It is the actual memories of the event that are important. Other people are involved with this event, but I am not in contact with them and probably will not be. I can't help but wonder what would happen if I ran into these people, now having a memory of an event that took place involving them, but no recollection of the event physically happening. All the while, knowing I am now in the Timeline where the event did in fact happen. An event that I know did not physically take place for me, when my Dominate Consciousness was residing in some other adjacent parallel reality. It matters not. I have strong memories of an event that I can still feel. And there is more than just one event that I am referring to. How is this possible?

Along the same lines, I have a memory that is really strange, that I am sure is impossible. My mother and father divorced when I was eight years old, and I have a younger brother and sister. With this memory, I am an only child and a female at that. That's right, the memory is of myself as a young, long haired blond, about fourteen years old, riding with my mother and father on the Disney monorail with my father telling me all about how the monorail would one day extend all the way to the hotel we were staying in. It is a vivid memory that is obviously impossible.

Jumping into another Timeline where the parameters are totally different can be unnerving, exciting, and confusing all at the same time. Just try to understand that when you jump Timelines you are not just changing your future; you have also changed your past. When I look back at a picture or video of myself. The further back I go, the less I recognize myself. This begs the question, 'Can we change our past, purposefully?' Why yes, we can! If we can shift our consciousness through parallel Timelines, then we can shift our consciousness to a reality where a past event is more to our liking. Simply immerse the memory with a similar memory yet more to your liking. It is more than just the memory. It is the emotion you bring with the memory. It is a vibrational frequency that you are aiming for. Like attracts like, so be and feel the way you want to be and feel. It is more involved than that, but as you start to focus on these ideas, it will become easier. It will become a knowing, and you will just Shift yourself into whichever Timeline you desire.

The Mandela Effect held my attention for many months. I was affected for sure, but even then, I was trying to justify away the many strange changes I was noticing. It was also around this time that I accidently clicked on a Flat Earth video. I sighed and decided to watch it to see what these people had to say. It was a video on explaining how the Earth could not be a globe and then they gave all of these mathematical reasons. I was lost immediately. They were also very sarcastic with their tones and inflections. I got over that quickly, as I could instantly bond with the passion this person had for his belief. But it was not going to draw me into the idea that the Earth was flat. So, I put it aside. But, not long after, maybe a couple of days, I again accidently clicked on another Flat Earth video, but this one was for beginners. It was dictated by a woman with two children. I could not believe it! This lady had the strength to blast out in public that she felt the Earth was flat. That only made me look deeper. And the deeper I looked, the more I was intrigued. I was not convinced at all. But I kept saying to myself, "Why not?" What if it was flat? Or maybe something else altogether. Maybe it is inverted? Maybe we are on the inside? How would I truly know? What about the Stars or the Sun and the Moon? And hold on, what of these Moon landings? Oh, so many questions. I mean, since I was born, I have been told that we live on a spinning globe that revolves around the Sun. And that that Sun is travelling at incredible speeds, flying through infinite space. If that is easy to believe than why couldn't we believe we live on an infinite plain or an infinite Realm or on the inside of a ball? What is the difference? The difference is your perception. And I was letting my perception become manipulated again. Remember, your perception is your reality.

I came across the idea that the South Pole was a barrier. The edge, as it were. The idea that Antarctica is the only continent that there has never been a war on is very impressive. And why not, since Antarctica has a peace treaty which includes all countries and that has got to make you blink. There is speculation that there is land on the other side of the Antarctic. Maybe that is where all of the young talented actors and musicians go when they die. Maybe Kurt Cobain, the artist formally known as Prince, and Randy Rhodes are all jamming together, somewhere over the rainbow. Some say giants live on the other side of the barrier. Or maybe the price you pay to be famous is to dine with the giants. And there are others who feel it is a barrier keeping us from the dome or firmament, as it is defined in the Bible. I found many things that were extremely interesting while investigating Flat Earth information. Yet, I was not convinced. But I was not going away, either. I was still engulfed in the Mandela Effect and since continents have been mentioned, let it be known that I do not recall Cuba being so close to the mouth of the Gulf of Mexico. I also do not remember the Bermuda triangle being at the tip of Florida. I always knew it to be further out at sea. Europe is off in many ways and there are other changes on the map that I have noticed but there are more qualified people and YouTube channels Like *Lone Eagle* or *NoblenessDee* that can verify the land mass differences, better than I can.

These things that I began questioning, no matter whether I received an answer divinely or not, was the start of me coming to the realization that I do not know, where we live or what we live in and/or on.

ANGELS, ORBS & MESSAGES

After the impalement experience, it seemed like everything changed. At least, that is when I really started to get excited. Not an excitement that I was comfortable with, but an excitement, nonetheless. Looking back now, I can say this is when I started to put some of the pieces together and seriously amuse myself by tinkering with the idea that death may be a catalyst to noticing Mandela Effects. Or what might actually be more accurate is, a Mandela Effect may be a sign that you died in another Timeline, and that your consciousness shifted into another Timeline with another physical body, etc. This idea did not come to fruition for many months. And when I did consider the idea seriously, my mind did what it apparently has been doing every time it comes across something that cannot be explained, it set it aside, it ignored it or it just explained it away by any means possible. It took watching a video from another YouTuber, whose channel name eludes me, who asked the question to get me to explore and appreciate that theory better. He asked something like, "Do all people who see the Mandela Effects die in another life?" When I answered the question in my head, it was a definite, yes! But how is that possible. This isn't what I thought death would be like. Or is it? I always thought after you shed the physical body, you go on living in whatever afterlife you focused on. So, is this heaven? Is this hell? The questions just kept pouring in and the answers were coming in by some strange means.

    My next aware bizarre experience happened about a month after the impalement, sometime in late June of 2015. That much, I am sure of. The date itself has shifted on me. Not to worry, you will understand what I mean by that, in time. What I did not realize at the time, was I was having other experiences, practically every day and they were connected. I just was not aware enough to recognize them. I was seeing more Mandela Effects, like changes in products, music and history. The thing was, I kept blowing most of these things off as me misremembering. I was not one hundred percent sure on many of them and the few I was absolutely sure of, I kind of put on the back burner. I knew something was up especially after the conversation with my ex-girlfriend and two of my best friends. Maybe I was not ready, or my mind was still trying to process the information. At any rate, these things would become more real to me and less of something faded, and that would be a couple of months before I was exposed to any Mandela Effect community.

I needed to find out what these experiences were. So, I decided to research the internet about the involvements I had with these things, but for now, I was still amazed at the unexplainable experiences I was having. Everything was truly being shown to me all at once, from my perspective. In the physical reality of time, it was over two years of experiences, both fascinating and mediocre, but all were bizarre none the less. This is about the time I started to visit a site where others were also noticing changes in history and pop-culture. The phenomenon known as The Mandela Effect was bigger and around longer than I expected. The term was coined by *Fiona Broome,* a paranormal investigator and author, who in 2010 became aware, along with many others, that Nelson Mandela became President of South Africa, after he died in prison. An interesting feat, to say the least. About a year later, I did find that there were others, prior to the Mandela Effect site, who were talking about the ability to Shift through timelines and that you could Shift your Consciousness into another reality. *Cynthia Sue Larson* started doing some great work on this subject back in 1999 and Burt Goldman also comes to mind. This idea of Shifting your Consciousness into other Timelines is the theory that I stand by, simply yet firmly, because of the many experiences I have had. Yet, at this time, I was just not ready to delve into that idea. I resonated with that theory better than any other theory that I had come across, so I kept it in the back of my mind that I would eventually study that further. The impalement incident was also in the back of my mind. It had occurred to me quite a few times that we may not die, that we may just Shift our Consciousness into another body or timeline or dimension, which was the term I was using at that time. But it was the Mandela Effect title, which was gaining momentum, so that is where my focus was.

Well, that night in June, I got home from work at the normal time, being approximately 3am. Normally, I would change clothes grab a beer or smoke some pot and sit at the computer, writing, working, studying or just surfing the web. But this night, I recall walking into my bedroom and nothing more. Nothing but waking up on my bed, fully dressed in my suit and tie. I did not think much of it at the time, as I was groggy from just waking after this short unexpected nap. But, looking back it seems very strange that I would lie down on the bed with my glasses and hat still on with a cigarette in my hand, ready to be lit.

Glancing at the clock I noticed it was 4:44am. A number I was seeing often around then and still now on occasion. I shuffled off the bed, grabbed a beer and a lighter and strolled to the door that would lead outside where I would have a bewildering experience, that I couldn't blow off as misremembering or glare or any other reason my mind would make up. This was real and amazing!

I walked to my normal spot to smoke my cigarette. I would stand in the backyard doorway of the one car garage, looking out towards the Colorado Rocky Mountains, at the stars. Directly in front of me, about three feet away, in the grass filled yard, was the football sized quartz crystal I acquired in the early nineties from a friend who told me its original home was in South Africa. It did not occur to me, until much later, that there may have been some significant to the crystals position in the lawn and the eye-opening experience, I was about to have.

Looking straight ahead at a brilliantly lit star, I just stood there enjoying the morning air. It was absolutely beautiful outside. Not a cloud in the sky and a temperate 70-ish degrees. My attention could not get off this star; it was angelic. It was bright and beautiful for sure, but it was my mind, my attention, my focus that was, for lack of a better explanation, in a daze. For absolutely no reason I can surmise, I purposefully pulled my attention away and I looked straight up. And there they were. Two gold-ish amoeba looking orbs, the size of cars and about forty yards over my head. Now, these things were angelic if I may. With my eyes looking at these orbs between the rim of my baseball cap and the rim of my glasses, I was sure this sight was not any type of glare. I backed up into the garage doorway and started looking back at the star that I first noticed. Wait!? What!? I am more interested in a star than these two translucent orbs?

Taking another step back, practically walking up the back of the garage door, I force my head back up, once again looking at these two gold orbs hovering over me. As soon as I locked my gaze, I began to get what I can only describe as a download. Honestly, I really do not know what it was, I just do not know how else to express the situation. I figure that download is as good of a description as any. It was like receiving a number of paragraphs loaded with information, in three seconds. There were no sounded words in my head or anything so physical, it was just a paragraph of information in one second and then another and another. I had to stop them. I did not absorb any of what they were trying to communicate. Even though I feel I got more than I know. The information slowed and what I recalled was maybe six key points in what they were trying to tell me. I have documented the main points. But here, what I want you to understand is, I had a cigarette in one hand and a beer in the other. I probably took a few hits of marijuana somewhere along the line, as well. What I received was things to do that would help me lift the veil. I didn't know this at the time, but it became obvious to me. It was apparent to me that the number one message to comprehend was to stop eating meat! It was not only the number one thing that they were trying to portray to me, but it was also number two on the list! It seemed obvious at the time that they really wanted me to stop eating meat. It was more about the energy for me than the meat itself. Number three was to refrain from releasing sexual energy. The impression I got was that it would be needed in my body. Number four, five and six seemed less important like refrain from gossiping, thinking and speaking correctly and so on. But these things were and are important too. Yes, what you might think would be on that list, is on that list. Why? Because whatever you are thinking right now is what would probably be on your list. Each person would have different things they would need to do or not do depending on how they have lived their lives. What I am saying is, if the orbs were to communicate to you about what you should do to experience more truth you may or may not have to do the things I was guided to do.

As I tried desperately to hide in the closed garage doorway, and being completely amazed at what I was seeing, I suddenly noticed the Orb on my left starting to dissipate. The one on the right finished up sending me impressions like, what they were, and who they were in relation to me and so forth, then dissipated as quickly as the other one did. The whole experience lasted no more than thirty seconds. I studied UFO's and aliens my whole life and have never seen one. I stood there in the doorway in shock, waiting for something to happen. Nothing but the beautiful night forcing itself back into my awareness. When I finally went back inside, I sat down and documented the experience.

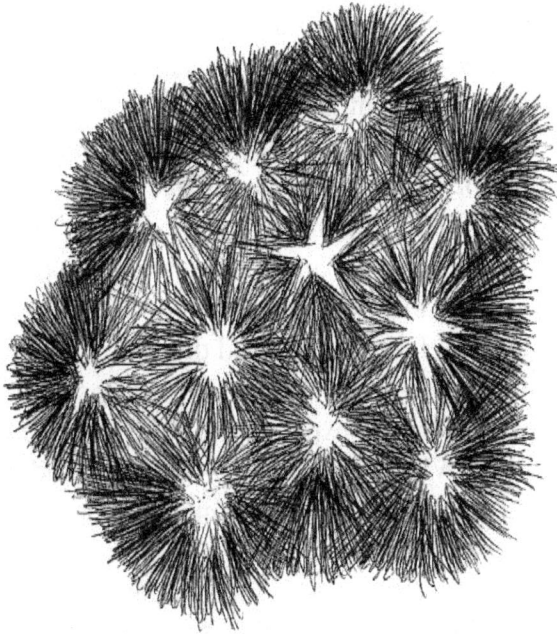

THE STARS

The first week, I attempted to stop eating meat. Well, I conveniently forgot that pepperoni and bacon were meat. You do not know how hard it is to stop eating meat, until you try. You do not realize how much meat you consume each day. Yet, when two orbs drop down and project in your mind to stop eating meat … you stop eating meat! The next two weeks were less than uneventful. I was having these little experiences weekly. Nothing too strong. But just enough to keep me muddled, questioning things and trying for the life of me to understand what in God's name was going on. Do not get me wrong, I was very excited and pleased that it seemed life was more than I thought, but a dreadful exciting feeling came from not knowing the territory in which I was exploring. I was looking for this stuff my whole life. I cannot count the nights I would just lie down, in whatever town I lived in, and stare at the stars. It is more than a reasonable reminiscence that I was reading something about the stars or life in other worlds. Oh, how grateful I am, to have had these experiences, which have torn me away from such nonsense. Most of the time, I would not realize I had an experience until it was over. Sometimes days later. With all of the things going on and with all of the thoughts running through my mind, my demeanor was one of solace, almost emotionless with a touch of calm.

All of that, would change in the coming months, as the questionable experiences would turn to obvious ones. The minor experiences I would categorize as something I could explain away easily. Then there were others that would make me realize these experiences are real. As the weeks moved on, I was becoming more and more intrigued by this whole Flat Earth movement. I felt, with the information I was exploring, that we were not living on a ball flying through space. I could not say if we lived on a Flat plain but that was where everyone else seemed to be heading and preaching, so that is the outlook I had upon it. But being flat? Although, in my opinion, that description is more accurate than a ball flying through space, it seemed like there was something more to this Flat Earth idea. The information I was reading on what the Egyptians believed, really held my attention. Mainly, because it was a completely different view from what I was used to, and I wasn't blowing it off as complete hogwash. It came to my attention that if the Stars were Souls, as they believed, then some part of us might be the Stars as well. I imagined that we are the stars projecting images of ourselves in this physical realm. I mean, why not? Now with this experience, these bright shining lights in the sky became more real to me. Throughout my life, I would star gaze on occasion. Now I was looking, staring and gazing every night. On this night in August, I was watching a Flat Earth video on the firmament, the Sun, moon and stars. Which, at the time, was my biggest question. If the Earth was flat and, in a dome, where are the stars, moon and sun? At this point, I would have still been on the fence with the whole Flat Earth idea, as it was definitely on my radar for months. Why was that? I was actually trying to picture the Earth as a flat dish or disk. I was putting my mind in a position where it would have to believe the Earth was flat and that we were all deceived for hundreds of years. Slowly but surely the pieces were falling into place. I am sure that it was a combination of things that brought me to the epiphany that sent me down a rabbit hole that I would never get out of. It wasn't just the recognition and realization that it was not going to be proven to me that we live on a ball, it was also the realization that it wasn't going to be proven to me that the Earth was flat. Everything I was studying pointed to the Earth not being a sphere spinning through space. The moon landings, for instance. From 1969 to 1972 the United States claimed to have been to and landed on the moon. This is also a Mandela Effect, with the number of landings being in question. Was it one or more? With the information I came across, it was proven to me that we not only never went to the moon, but we have never left the atmosphere. I did not stop there. How could you? My next question about the deception on the moon would have to wait, as my consciousness woke up and the awareness hit me all at once. My mind was racing all over the place. The epiphany that hit me strong was that nothing was going to be proven to me. Nothing could be proven to me. Everything I believed was told to me and I accepted it without question. The heaviest weight I have ever known was lifted from my entire body. My mind was open and clear for the first time in this physical body. I had to take a break. I grabbed a cigarette and headed outside.

It was a dark clear night on August 8th, 2015, just before midnight. I was overly excited! I felt free just speculating that the earths shape could not be proven to me. The energy level was off the charts. I could not believe what I was feeling. It was amazing and freeing. I could not wait to stare at the stars. As I write this, I am reminded of the epiphanies and feelings that were rushing through my body. I cannot express to you how much I want to have and enjoy this experience again. As I walked out to the middle of the yard, I pulled my lighter to my cigarette and lit it. I turned around and looked up at the stars. With my cigarette tucked between my fingers, I raised my hand and with a rainbow-like motion I threw my arm across the sky and shouted out loud, "I bet you're all just UFO's". And that's when my perception of life changed …

The stars responded immediately. The first one was the most shocking. It came right at me. In a split second, this one star extended itself towards me. It became larger and brighter and it was directed right at my chest. I froze. It is not like I could have moved out of the way. I do faintly recall, that for the smallest amount of measurable time, I thought this was it, I was going to die. And, I did not even have time to review my life. With absolutely no time to think, make a decision or run, I accepted my fate. It came right up to me, maybe a foot or less away. And then, as quickly as this bright star came upon me, it retracted itself back to its original position. And then, more stars did the same extension as movement, all directed at my heart. After the initial wave they started do other things. Thinking back on it now and writing this here, I feel that the first star, was a kind of signal to get my attention or an overture, if you will. In all, it was seven to nine stars and maybe more, dancing in the night sky, all directed at me from different directions. I was still frozen. I didn't dare move. I pulled my glasses down to see if there would be a difference. There was no difference. If anything, they seemed more real, although not as clear. My first thought was that I didn't want them to see me. But it wasn't just me that I didn't want them to see.

This is an interesting topic in itself and should be categorized under my cleansing. As I looked up at this beautiful amazing sight, I started to bring my left hand down as to block the cigarette. It has not dawned on me until very recently, while talking with a few of my trusted Mandela affected friends, *Photohelix* and *Scarabperformance*, who I only know from communicating with them on YouTube and talking with them on the telephone, that there was a reason for my embarrassment about holding onto a cigarette. I would not dare put that thing to my mouth while these angelic, biblical, intelligent, wondrous beings were, communicating with me or doing whatever it was that they were doing with me. So, why was I embarrassed to have a cigarette? They must see me now and possibly all the time, assuming time is anything like it is here in the physical realm. And now, that I think about it, I feel it would be more plausible for me to infer that they, the stars, placed themselves into the physical dimension and time, to communicate with me. And if that is the case, well I can see where my embarrassment stems from. I feel smoking cigarettes, even if they do not affect me the way they affect most people, was not in my original program. Anytime a doctor took a stethoscope to my chest, he or she would move that thing everywhere they could and would always ask, if I smoked. Strange since I would answer that yes, I smoke, on their questionnaire coming in the door every time. I swear they had problems locating my heart. If anything, I was probably programmed not to smoke cigarettes before I was born. I can feel that. Hence, my embarrassment with the stars.

At night for many years, I would feel this irregular heartbeat that no doctor would ever acknowledge. I did not then, nor do I now believe in the need for doctors, for myself. But there were times where it just could not be avoided. You may vibrate a different way so please if you feel you need a doctor for something please by all means do what you feel is best. But, with experience comes wisdom, and I say just shift your consciousness out of that situation. Yes, I do believe it is that simple. But of course and as always, please get advice from your doctor before you shift your consciousness into another Timeline and be aware that the side effects include some slight misremembering.

It was actually closer to the year 2000 when I realized I had a strange feeling in my chest. It was almost euphoric. Every so often and only while I was lying down in bed, I would notice my breathing pattern would change. It would be normal and then nothing. The air was building up in some vein or something. And then it would push through and this euphoric sensation would flood over my body. This would happen almost every night until I would fall asleep. This is significant, as after this experience, I no longer felt that sensation in my heart and have not felt it since. Interestingly enough, I do recall feeling that sensation after the impalement, even though the heart changed location on me after that experience.

I quickly realized that since the stars were directing themselves at me from many different directions, they knew I was there. I still did not dare move. My second thought was that I did not want them to stop. I could have stood there all night, just gazing at these beautiful lights shifting and dancing, or were they communicating? If it was a message of some sort, with the adrenaline running through my veins, I was not going to hear it while being in the moment. I was too busy searching for my phone. At this point, it was about a minute and a half into the adventure and my phone was nowhere to be found. I searched every pocket twice, not taking my eyes off of the stars and their spectacle. I stood there another minute with the cigarette burning in my fingers. It was amazing, beautiful, exciting, impossible and exhilarating and so many more emotions, feelings and wonders I did not know existed. I started to walk towards the house, thinking my phone would be right on the other side of the door. As I did, the stars slowed their formations. So, I stopped, and they sped up. I decided to try and communicate. I wish I would have thought this out better, but who has time to think things out when the stars are dancing for you? I said out loud, "If this is just for me to see, when I get back, with my phone to record this, you'll stop."

Seriously, what was I thinking? I took a good look at the stars and then ran into the house. I looked around for no more than three seconds and really felt like I needed to be back outside. Again! What was I thinking? I ran as fast as I could back to the yard where the stars showed themselves to me and … nothing. Nothing, but the normal beautiful stars I would gaze upon every so often. As I stretched my eyes across the sky, my free hand went to my side and I felt what could only be my phone. I stayed outside for a while longer, hoping the light extravaganza would transpire again, but to no avail.

Maybe an hour or so went by when I decided to write down my experiences with more detail. All of them. I started with the freshest, the stars. The notes I took, as detailed as I thought I was being at the time, seemed to be more of an outline. The same goes for all of the other documented material. Not only that, but some of the dates are simply wrong, vague, meaning just the month is presented or just off a bit from what I recall. Some of the material, I think to myself, "Wow, I wrote that?" and have no recollection of it and other things I recall, as I am reading along.

So, how did I interpret this experience? This event showed me that the Stars are not Suns with Planets revolving around them and that the Earth may in fact, not be a sphere. The epiphany was strong, and I felt the most amazing weight lifted from my chest. And that was the point. It really did not matter if the Earth was a Ball or a Pancake, it was the idea that something I truly believed in, something I would never question, was wrong, false and/or a lie. At least, that is how I felt at the time. How would you have interpreted that most astounding, life changing experience? My interpretation comes from the fact that I was studying Egyptian writings and how they believed the Stars were Souls and at the same time watching and reading as much Flat Earth material as I could. This is where my focus was, and that focus was bombarded with emotion. Another ingredient for shifting your Consciousness to something more to your liking.

Weeks went by, and still not tethered to time, my views on the shape of the planet were zeroing in on that we did not live on a spinning globe, revolving around a Sun, that was also rotating around a Central Sun. I fell into the trap of stating that I felt the Earth was flat, when in fact, I did not know and still do not know now, what the shape is. I strongly lean towards it is about your perception and does not matter what the shape is, except for the fact that our money is being taken from us because of lies to control the masses. But this is also your perception. What I was leaning towards, was that we are not living on a ball flying through the vacuum of Space. At least, that is what I have come to feel after the experience with the stars. Yet, even with all of the experience, truth and belief can still change.

About a month after having the stars perform their light show, I was surfing through YouTube information and I spotted a video where a woman was zooming in on stars with a Nikon P900 camera. Well, imagine my shock when the stars looked extremely similar to the orbs that hovered over my head a few months back. Is that what these intelligent beings look like up close? Can they come through the firmament or the barrier that may separate us from the waters above? Are they inside the dome or firmament? So many exciting questions. But most would have to wait. The only one that I would focus on was the one that mattered most. What was I seeing? The stars that were zoomed in on looked remarkably similar to the Orbs, yes, but there were also differences. I do not know what I saw in either case, but one thing is for sure, there is an intelligence at work.

WHEN COMES

The rest of the week went by with me looking up more material on the Flat Earth and contemplating what had happened to me during my experience with the stars. I really had no answer, except that my world was literally turned upside-down. Or would that be squashed? For the longest time afterward, I would just see what others had to say about the Flat Earth material. I bought right into it, after totally ignoring it. After all, it is what changed my perception of reality, right?

Why wasn't it the Mandela Effect? I mean physical reality is changing all around me and I go for the more tangible conspiracy theory? That is not like me. A supernatural, paranormal experience is what I had and definitely more of what I am geared or programmed to explore. Being exposed to the Mandela Effect and being affected by it changed my way of thinking for sure yet studying Egyptian beliefs and Flat Earth material triggered the experience I had with the Stars and that changed my perception of reality. It is all connected. It really did not matter if I believed the Earth was flat, it was the idea that I realized that I didn't know what it was. I was told a lie my whole life. That much I knew. But what was I to do with that?

One beautiful afternoon in mid-August, I was out in the yard looking up into the sky and my eye caught a flock of small birds, maybe two hundred yards in the air. As I watched them, I noticed a peculiar pattern. The pattern was sporadic, in that they all flew forward for a spell, then it looked as though they would disappear, fly back and to the right a short distance and then forward again. The disappearing, I attributed to the sun glaring off of the bird's wings. Since then, I have speculated that if we reside in a computer simulation, which is one of the more plausible theories, there was a glitch of some sort. This went on for a good five minutes. I could not take my eyes off of them, until I heard one of my roommates open the backdoor. He came outside and we extended the normal pleasantries. The entire conversation took no longer than twenty seconds. As he was walking back into the house, I got excited to get back to my birds. I looked up and they were gone. I looked in every direction they could have flown and nothing. They could not have gone that far at all. The time that elapsed while I was watching them fly all over the place and still keep their direction was a little more than five minutes and even then, they had not reached my position.

It was strange little experiences like this that I more than likely just blew off as misremembering something or seeing something wrong. How many times have you said that your eyes were playing tricks on you? How many times have you misplaced something knowing where you left it? And how many times have you asked a friend about a movie you both saw together, and they don't know what you're talking about? Maybe, you witnessed or experienced a Shift.

Before I knew it, September was upon me. The Mandela Effect Site had chatter about September 23rd. It was all I was waiting for. As later I would come to realize, these things or shifts are nothing to wait for. Prepare and go get it! I would occasionally check out Mandela Effect videos. As mentioned, at first, I was not completely sure about most of them, but it really only takes one Mandela Effect that you are absolutely one hundred percent sure of, to be tempted to slide down the rabbit hole. Even so, most of them I was not sure about. Also as mentioned, the first one that I was exposed to, and not affected by, was the Berenstain Bears change in spelling. For me, the affect was that they existed at all. Although my mind fought like hell to justify being affected by several of the noticeable changes, it was the undeniable changes, the changes that I knew were impossible, that pulled me down the rabbit hole. *Interview with a/the Vampire, Sex in/and the City, Jiffy* peanut butter and of course *Mirror/Magic Mirror on the Wall,* are just a few of the Mandela Effects, I could not get over. And the two biggest Mandela Effects for me have not even transpired yet or maybe they just were not noticed yet. At this time, the Mandela Effect was growing at an incredible rate, yet I did not know this until I visited a web site called *mandelaeffect.com*. The site was created by *Fiona Broome* who, for over forty years, has been an author, researcher, and paranormal consultant. Here is an excerpt from the site, describing how the name Mandela Effect came into being.

"Many years ago, I was one of the two people who coined the phrase 'Mandela Effect' during a conversation in Dragon Con's 'green room.' Between speaking to audiences, many of us would start discussions about quirky fun topics. It was a way to relax. (The other person was called 'Shadow,' then a Dragon Con security manager. I have no idea which one of us started using the phrase, first. And, it's possible that my husband came up with the phrase. It was a typical, informal, not-very-serious 'what if...?' conversation in that room.) The discussion started when Shadow mentioned that - like me – other people remembered Nelson Mandela's tragic death in a South African prison prior to late 2009. (In this reality, Mandela died in 2013.) Apparently, others in the green room shared that memory. Many others joined the conversation. It was a fascinating discussion that spun into weird and hilarious tangents. After retuning home, I researched the concept that started this website to see how widespread the Mandela memories were. I thought it was an interesting fringe topic (and potential book topic) for my spare

time. Since then, this topic has turned into something much bigger. I'm still astonished by that." – Fiona Broome

The Mandela Effect site became a safe haven for me. I had no problem going out into the physical world and opening my mouth to talk with people in public about my experiences. It was the negative responses and feedback that started to unnerve me. I needed a place I could go and discuss what I and others were noticing without being ridiculed. Fiona's site gave me that. I remember first getting on the site and not knowing where I should start. I started reading whatever was on the home page but the information I hoped to find was just a bit deeper. I came across the 'Memories' page and started on the first thread. I could do nothing but read. Since my cell phone was my only means of communication with media, I was glued to it, not stopping for anything.

At this point, I was totally affected by the Mandela Effect, and that is where my focus was. I read, I slept, and I ate. One meal a day is all it seemed I needed. Five hours of sleep at night, if that, was all that my body could take. And that, is all that took place that first week. And, as exciting as it was for me to be in contact with other people who have had similar experiences and memories, it was a seemingly uneventful space of time, considering what would happen within the next two weeks.

Each morning, I would wake myself up to enjoy the day immediately! It was always the most beautiful haze. Foggy, yet temperate. You'll understand better, when you understand what it was that I was going through during the nights.

I was in a unique situation because I was not working during these experiences. I took a voluntary layoff from work.

Strange as I have never been without a job before. And it would be just like me to make sure I was not involved with anything or anybody while these experiences were taking place. This did give me the unknown positive opportunity of not being tethered to time. Which, looking back, had a lot to do with my experiences and how I interpreted them.

The first night I started reading on the Mandela Effect site, the air or feeling around me started to feel thick. This description is an afterthought; at the time I was zeroed in on the subject at hand and had no idea I may have shifted into another Timeline. It was around June of 2015 when this shifting theory showed up. It was on the Mandela Effect site, and with all of the research going on there, a list of theories was inevitable.

Anyway, that first night of reading was very intense. After deciding to read through the fifteen threads, which had approximately two hundred and fifty comments in each thread, I situated myself where my broken computer sat and dove in. I read about half of the first thread and decided to join the website, as there were many Mandela Effects I wanted to comment on. I started to post comments and replies on this site, under the name 'Anthony'.

At some point that night, I started to feel strange. It wasn't a feeling of being sick, which would come later; it was more like a weight lifting from my body, but it was a dark, dense feeling that was not pleasant by any means. I recall letting it happen and not fighting it. This had something to do with the thread I was reading. It was seriously blowing my mind. I didn't care what was happening, I just wanted it to happen. And well, I got my wish. I could feel what might be described as evil leaving my body. Looking back and understanding what I do now, it is probably more accurate to say that the lies I have been told my whole life were leaving my body, as my mind was desperately trying to understand and accept these lies, rather than accept the truth. The truth was, I didn't know what the truth was anymore. This process was going to take some time.

The next day I was searching 'The Wall' on YouTube as the phrase 'The Wall' kept synchronistically coming up for me while I was exploring Flat Earth material, Egyptian beliefs on Stars and The Mandela Effect phenomenon. It was about dusk when I had the stove on in the other room and just as I was about to get up to check on my boiling water for spaghetti, a YouTube feed comes up on my cell phone, with a complete black screen. I hit it. It is all static and inaudible. A deep voice creeps through the static, 'we call it the wall, it has been broken, it is a shifting of dimensions', or something extremely similar. I was very intrigued. So, I hit pause, figuring I would take care of the boiling water and come back to really listen and concentrate on what was being said. When I got back to my room, I grabbed my phone, which is where I was watching YouTube videos at this time, since my personal computer had been destroyed. I hit the play button and nothing, it was gone. There was no hint of this being on the screen and there was nothing in my history. I am still not sure what that was all about. It gave me motivation to continue to research, but what was it? Who was it, how did they communicate with me and why inform me? I am grateful, no doubt. It just seemed like a very personal and direct phenomenon.

It was also around this time while exploring the phrase 'The Wall' that the word 'Brick' on the Pink Floyd album sounded like 'Break' to me, and still does to this day. It may also be worth mentioning a discovery from YouTuber Hazel Fiver, that there may be a discrepancy with the group's name.

It seems the group's name may have Shifted. Does "The Pink Floydd" look right to anyone?

It was within the next few days when the physical pain started. My back and legs were stiff and feverish. I felt awful, yet I continued reading. Crouched in the corner of my room with my football sized quartz at my side, feeling protected by the walls around me helped relieve the feeling of paranoia. I felt like I was being watched by something unseen or invisible. I knew it was there. I had the feeling that it was simply curious as to what I was reading. So, I sat back and opened my arms. I did not actually see anything with my eyes but what I felt was both frightening and relieving! If I can say I sensed a presence, which would be more accurate, then I would say I sensed an entity become very irate and leave the area. Not the room, just the immediate vicinity I was located. It was not long after this I started to see something shoot out from one end of the room to the other, out of the corner of my eyes. This became a frequent occurrence as I read.

I would take short five-minute breaks here and there and lie down on the bed with one of my quartz crystals. This seemed to take any pain away almost immediately. I got the idea from an *Abraham Hicks* video, stating to stay close to your crystals. At first, I was just using it for the little headaches I was getting. This was strange in itself as I do not ever remember getting a random headache. Now, I was getting them often.

It was around this time when I came across a thread that stated many believed there used to be fifty-two states in the United States of America. I thought, what do they mean by 'used to be'? Oh, there are only fifty states. Now I do recall fifty-two states. But it was a foggy young memory and I could not be sure. I decided to distract myself and sat to watch some *'Star Trek The Next Generation'*. I was watching an episode called 'The Royal'. Right in the beginning of the episode they were showing a flag with fifty-two stars. Granted this is science fiction and based in the future, so any justification could have been defined. But the fact that I just got done reading threads on this subject seemed too coincidental. So, I watched this episode intently, during which I found what seemed to be clues that the other two states were part of Texas. Without getting into details here, I wrote a comment on the mandelaeffect.com site explaining my findings. I deduced that this episode showed Texas as three states. North Texas, Central Texas and West Texas. This idea was also hinted at in a television show called *Fringe*.

The third and fourth days went along the same way, with the exception that I was becoming more aware of many things. The veil was lifting. My body felt lighter and I felt freer. Yet, I was still bound to physical reality. Of course, at the time I was still unaware that the theories I would postulate would become my reality. I was reading more than I was exploring videos. I tried to mix up the topics on videos when I would watch, while keeping it esoteric and supernatural. I came across some videos that were theorizing that we are coming into a five-dimensional existence. That we are evolving to a higher vibration and becoming five dimensional beings. Some interpret that as their higher-self coming into embodiment. Other theories I came across were that CERN was controlling the Mandela Effect Phenomenon or trying to control it. That the D-Wave computer was causing all of the changes in history. That we are in a computer simulation and that program has been infected with a virus. Time Travel came up a few times and still does. And even with the many other theories I walked into, the top theory on my list, and one that I brought up on the Theories Page on the Mandela Effect site, was that we are Multidimensional beings experiencing

Multiple Timelines and it is Natural. We are far behind where we should be. Our lives have been suppressed, whether we did it to ourselves on purpose or not. Shifting seems natural to me and I feel we should be shifting or creating as needed. The theory I have formulated and tweaked would be that it is Our Consciousness that Shifts through different timelines based on our focus, feeling and intent and maybe a verbal Intent. Yet, this too could just be terms used and we could be shifting from program to program.

In 2006, I spoke with psychic *Dannion Brinkley*. During that enlightening conversation, he described to me what we as human beings would be experiencing in the near future. I believe his terminology was that we are multidimensional beings and will be experiencing multiple dimensions. This conversation is as much the reason for my terminology and understanding, as well as the experiences themselves.

THE FORD SHIFT

It was early October of 2015 when I had an experience
with shifting into one dimension and returning back to what
would be accurately described as returning to a dimension
closer in relation to the one, I left.

I was on foot and headed to the local cigar shop to
watch a football game. I was aware that spectator sports were
one of the many distractions that keep us from knowing truth,
but after all of the experiences I was having, I needed a break.
Looking back, I gathered what I felt and experienced, I did not
fully understand until I left the cigar shop and contemplated
the experience. The second I walked through the cigar shop
door; a wave of energy hit me. The room felt dark, dank and

unfamiliar. My mind was not focused on how the room felt at this time. I just picked a cigar and sat in a chair to watch the game. I also recall that it seemed like everyone was looking at me. Paranoid? There was pizza offered and the piece I took could have been three days old. The New York Giants were playing the Denver Broncos and it was the fourth quarter, near the end of the game, when a commercial came on that caught my attention. It was a Ford truck commercial. The top of the 'F' in Ford logo, had a very gaudy long curly-Q. It took up most of the screen and really did not look right at all. I could not help but wonder if this wasn't one of those Mandela Effects. After the game I checked every car logo I passed looking for the FORD symbol. The few I came across had a small curly-Q in the middle of the 'F', but not the top. I thought this strange, but even stranger was that I did not recall the small curly-Q, however I convinced myself that it was there before. When reporting this event on the mandelaeffect.com site, I stated that the small middle curly-Q was there. To this day, I have not seen the top of the 'F' in the Ford logo have a curly-Q. And apparently the small little curly-Q in the middle of the 'F has always been there, as since then, I have been to a few car shows and all of these really old Ford cars have the same curly-Q.

Something else I did that felt curious was that I checked the score of the football game, assuming that if I jumped Timelines the score might be different. The score was the same. Even still, looking back at this experience, I could feel how different the air was. The vibration was different. It was almost as if the people in the cigar shop were looking at me like I just left or like they knew me. When I left the cigar shop it was very cloudy and hazy, like it has been for that whole month and some. And it was like a bright shiny day in my heart as I walked out the cigar shop door. These feeling did not hit me until much later, after the experience. And I am often reminded of this experience as the Ford logo has changed five times for me since 2015. The way it looks now, is how it has looked throughout 'this' history.

While writing about this event, I decided to do a little research. I knew it took place sometime in the fall before the Blood Moon, but I wanted the date. I have told the story many times and I have written about it at least three times. I have always said that I was watching the Broncos play the Giants. I recall that vividly. I also recall that I took note of the score, thinking it might change when I looked at it later. The final score was 23-20 Broncos. While researching, I discovered that the Vikings lost to the Broncos that day 23-20. This is a Personal Mandela Effect for me. I did not have to relay that information. I could have simply changed the Giants to Vikings, and no one would know the difference. Why? Because when I researched my comments on the Mandela Effect site, it seems I mention that I took note of the score, but I mentioned nothing about who played. I find that strange. Since the event took place, I have stated that the Broncos were playing the Giants.

What did this experience teach me? If we do in fact Shift our Consciousness from one Timeline to another Timeline to experience motion and time, it seems as though we can move in and out of other Dimensions. When we apply ourselves with the proper formula, which honestly must conform to not being a formula, I truly feel we can travel through time and other dimensions, to say nothing of flying and not physically aging. I honestly do not know how that would work with age and the physical body, but that is one of the many ideas I have taken away from this and other experiences. One day soon, human beings may be flying without the aid of machines.

SPELLING MISSISSIPPI

Besides some mentioned past events, all of these experiences happened in the state of Colorado. My last experience in Colorado, this time around, was interesting in itself. I went to my old roommate's apartment to visit because I knew I would be leaving the state soon. I started telling him about the Mandela Effect and he just kept laughing. I could not understand his reaction until he told me he knew about the Mandela Effect back when we were roommates. After he explained his reluctance to talk with anyone about it, we slowly got into the conversation. He showed me a tapestry that we always talked about when I lived there. It was Eastern Indian in fashion and all of the positive symbols and words were on the right side of the tapestry and all of the negative words and symbols were on the left side. Now as I looked at it, I noticed right away that the colors were more vibrant, and the outlines were more direct. It took a minute, but I eventually realized that the positive and negative words and symbols were all mixed up. This is when we both started talking up a storm. He broke out a *Grateful Dead* pin called *Steal Your Face* that he bought the previous year. He set the pin down on the coffee table while he looked up the pin online. As he was looking for the pin, my eyes started playing tricks on me. The red and blue colors kept switching sides. I yelped out loud and he looked and saw it change as well. We took pictures and compared the pins and according to this reality, the one he bought last year, never existed.

It was in late November and into December of 2015 that I moved to Mississippi for a job. My goal was to run a casino and run it properly. I was moving up in the casino business over the years and believed I acquired a position that would put me in the direction to achieve my desire. What I did not know at this time, and what is a very important ingredient in creating the physical reality you desire, is that I didn't quite express my desire properly. What I mean to say, is for me, my desire was too descriptive. I needed to be vaguer.

Can I interject at this time and express the confusion over the word 'vaguer'. Is that really a word? I initially wrote the line as, 'I needed to be more vague, but the spell check instantly changed the phrase to vaguer. Many words seem to have changed their spelling over night as well. And that tends to be a *dilemna*. This I noticed while editing my *"Paul McCartney"* documentary. A lot; *alot;* allot; all three words at one time or another seemed to be words. And now *alot* seems to not be a word once again. Somewhere around the year 2000, I called my sister-in-law who is an English teacher and I asked her how to spell the word, 'a lot'. She proceeded to tell me that it is actually two words, 'a' and 'lot'. I accepted this as truth and went back to my "Paul" documentary and changed all of the, *alot's* to 'a lot'. Back to the present a little, when I was reading up on Mandela Effects, one site or another talked about how, a lot can be expressed three ways. The idea here is that *alot* was a word, then was not a word and back and forth again. I am discovering now as I write this, that *alot* is not a word, again. Who knows what it will be by the time you read this.

Enough digression. My first experience in Mississippi was a bit different than the earlier more supernatural experiences. I must say now that one thing that definitely changed was my diet. My diet went from no meat at all to shrimp and turkey. I couldn't help but wonder if there was a connection as the experiences, I had in Mississippi were less intense, if you will.

I was strolling down a street looking for something to eat that did not contain meat. I had Mandela Effects on my mind, as I felt that the experiences seemed to change or became less dramatic. On my way to the Burger King, (I am sure they have a veggie burger, right?), a few blocks away, I glanced across the street at a sign that read *"Collectibles"*, well I started to freak out because I knew one hundred percent that the word was spelled *"Collectables"*. I was pretty excited when I grabbed my phone to explore this change. Would you believe the search engine explained that the word could be spelled both ways? Now, with this sort of experience I have hypothesized that it could be two or more different Timelines or Dimensions merging.

Disappointed with the internet's explanation on the word *"Collectibles"*, I shuffled on to Burger King. I was fighting the urge to walk in as I made my way to the door. I put my hand on the door and started to open it when I noticed that it looked fairly busy. That stopped me! I did not want to eat meat anyway, so I left and devoured a veggie hoagie from Subway a block away. That part of the story may seem bland at best until you realize the following week, I was driving by that same Burger King and they were building it. The foundation was the only thing there and the following day walls were up. I was sure I put my hand on the door and saw people inside, the week before. Yet, as you may recall at this point when I was in Mississippi and the experiences took a turn, I was justifying anything that came my way. Not on purpose, it is just what I was doing. But not so much with this experience. I tried to convince myself that it was the Dairy Queen next door. Nope, I could not do it. I knew what I saw. I was not going to buy my own bullshit this time. Something was forcing me back down the rabbit hole.

A week later I was explaining to a friend where I lived, as he was going to come by and watch a game. As I was explaining where I lived, he interrupted me by asking, isn't that right down the street from the Burger King? And I replied, "Yes, the new one they are building". And he said no, the one that has been there for two years. I just let it go rather than argue or try to explain. It was a good thing I did not argue. As I drove home that day, I decided to go a bit further to see how far they were with the construction on the new Burger King. Well, that was quick. It was up and running at full speed. I went in this time. As I cased the place with my eyes, I seem to remember the counter being on the opposite side. No matter. I order a fish sandwich and sat down at a random table. Directly to my left, I see an article talking about the first burger sold and eaten two years ago, at this Burger King. It seems, some man for some reason has had the first burger in the last five or so new Burger Kings in Mississippi.

It was also around this time that I was questioning my ideas about the earth being flat. I believed we lived on a ball flying through space. I believed that NASA landed on the moon. Both I believed because that is what I was taught and told. And now, I was doing the same thing all over. I was taking other people's ideas that the Earth was flat and accepting it. This started to bother me, and I started questioning everything. I stayed with the Flat Earth concept, as it was more to the truth of what I really felt at this time, that we are not on a sphere spinning through infinite space. But, as far as it being flat, I really did not know, but I would talk with others about it anyway. I soon realized I had no proof, only what I was hearing from others. I really did not know and that started to creep up on me.

I disliked living in Mississippi. Granted it was for a job. Not only that but by the second month there, I was being harassed at work, reporting it and having nothing done about it. The details are unimportant here but during an interview for a promotion, I was told that believing the Earth was Flat was not going to help me get the promotion. At the time I labeled it as '*Flat Earth*,' when I spoke about it. I would correct myself by saying, "I don't know what it is but because of the experiences I have had, I strongly feel we do not live on a globular planet spinning through space at unfathomable speeds." That concept sounds like a joke to me now. But it is important for me to come to terms with myself and state that I do not know what it is and neither do you. You only believe what you have been told by the authorities because you have been programmed to know it is so impossible for authority to lie and manipulate. 'Flat Earth' is a terrible title for that awakening or movement. All the Flat Earth community has done is opened up a can of worms that, quite frankly, needed to be opened. For me it helped me Shift my reality or more accurately, Shift my Perception. Other ideas that go along with the Flat Earth concept are that we are in a dome or that there is more land on the other side of the South Pole. How can one be sure the Earth is flat without actually experiencing it, after you just witnessed what happens when you assume everything you are told is truth?

The friend I spoke of earlier who would be my roommate, a man I knew for over thirty years, was totally unaffected by the Mandela Effect. Truth is, he had to listen to me talk about conspiracies his whole life, why should this one be any different? Things just are the way they are, and you have to enjoy yourself, end of story. That was his motto. Weird that I have a memory of attending his funeral back in 2014. Not a strong memory but a memory not a dream or made up imagined story. Yet, I did not have this memory when I lived with him for a few months in 2015. It was during that time that we lived together that I pushed talking about the Tiananmen Square incident and he clearly recalled the man being run over and then just having his foot run over, and then his expression changed. I saw what was happening. He was having multiple memories, not just a dual memory. I don't recall the rest of the conversation, but by the time we were finished, he was sure the man was run over in some way and was very surprised when seeing the video of the man jumping up on the tank.

After that episode, I had the pleasure of being alone for a week and that is really when I had most of the experiences down in Mississippi. This week alone, turned out to be continually active.

The mildest experience I had in Mississippi happened on a beautiful morning and it was not the only experience I had that day. I went out to on the balcony to have a cigarette and some coffee. I sat down and lit the cigarette, taking a few drags. Looking for my coffee I realized I left it inside. When I came back with the coffee, the cigarette showed no signs of ever being lit. It sat in the ashtray, a fresh cigarette.

That same day, I noticed the sign across the street had changed. I cannot be sure, but I think I was on to this before this event took place. The establishment across the street, some sort of work-out facility, had its name and phone number fastened to the side wall outside. I noticed this many weeks earlier because not all of the numbers and letters were showing. It seemed that some of them had fallen down. Well, some of the letters and numbers that were down the day before were now up and others looked as though they had fallen or came unfastened. This happened several times over the next couple of months.

One day, off of the same balcony, I noticed a *FORD* dealership two blocks away. This I took notice of because of the obvious *FORD* symbol change. Across from the dealership was a lot where they parked their overflow of cars. The next day the lot where the cars were parked, was a small strip mall complete with Pizza Store and Nail Salon.

The most unnerving experience also took place in Mississippi. One afternoon I decided to call my daughter, who lived in New York at the time. I wanted to chat with her about a Mandela Effect that I thought she may resonate with. I had mentioned the Mandela Effect once or twice to her but if there was any acknowledgement, I am sure she was just appeasing her father. To her, it was just one more crazy conspiracy I was into. The conversation was short, but long enough to have a very strange experience. She answered her phone saying she could not talk as she was with her girlfriend in a Starbucks coffee shop and they were in the middle of important work. I said, Okay and she stopped me stating that her girlfriend left for the restroom. "What's up?" she asked. I replied telling her that I was looking at some of the Mandela Effects people were talking about and if she remembered Louis Anderson. And she replied in the affirmative saying, yes, the guy that hosted Family Feud and died.

What happened next was strange in itself and I did not really react as if it were. When I told her he was still alive, at first, she was like no way, and then it was like she mixed him up with someone else. It was almost like talking to two different people. Then she went on about how it sounded like a movie she recently saw, but she could not remember the title of the movie. She said there was a woman that kept feeding her dead father spaghetti. I pushed her for the title of the movie, but she just could not recall it. All of a sudden, the connection went a little haywire. We could still hear each other; it is just that there was a bit of static. She stopped the conversation by stating that her girlfriend was back from the restroom and that she really had to go. We said goodbye. I remember feeling very tired and taking a short nap right after the call.

The next afternoon I went off to the library to check out some movies. I went right to the Sci-Fi section and grabbed the first 'Star Trek' reboot, 'Batman Begins' and 'Prometheus'. I figured that was enough to keep me distracted. As I was leaving the last aisle a movie box caught my eye. I don't recall why but I took it from the shelf and upon reading the back and seeing that Anthony Hopkins was in it I decided to give it a shot, even though it was not my normal *Cup O' Soup*. The movie was called, "*Proof*". Now, the title was about a paper, not proof of anything for me. Or was it?

I put the movie '*Proof*' in first. A few minutes into the movie I realized I knew the dialogue and I also knew that it was impossible for me to know anything about this movie except for what was written on the back. I started to say the dialogue out loud. It freaked me out a bit, to be sure. I paused the movie and just froze staring at the screen in horror for a good ten minutes. I finally got up the nerve to hit play. The movie went along smoothly from there for a while, and I realized I was not sure what was going to happen, and I had to pay attention to the plot. As soon as I felt comfortable enough to sit back and enjoy the movie, I started blurting out the dialogue again, and it was still unintentional and impossible, as I did not know the dialogue.

"I'm glad he's dead." I said, right along with the girl on the screen and grabbed the remote control and hit pause once again. I figured I would scrummage around for some food. I needed a break from all of the relaxing. After a turkey sandwich and some chips, I decided to try this movie '*Proof*', once more.

So, if you think this is a bit strange so far, you will be as shocked as I was when, a few more minutes into the movie, and this woman was feeding her dead father spaghetti! Wait one minute! What?!? How is this possible? Do you believe in coincidences? Even if you do believe in coincidences, the odds of me randomly picking out a movie that was only described to me, with the genre and everything else involved, must be ridiculously huge! Could this get any stranger?

I actually watched the whole movie before calling my daughter to tell her about the incredible coincidence that took place. I wanted to call right away but I was too glued to the movie after that scene. And let us not forget that the movie is called, "*Proof*".

The conversation was on a downward spiral right from the beginning. I started telling her how I randomly picked out the movie she described, and that this girl was feeding her dead father spaghetti. She seemed like she was with me at first but then she stopped me and asked to repeat some of the things I said that she had no idea what I was talking about. So, I continued with, "You know, the movie you told me about yesterday, the one where the girl is feeding her dead father spaghetti and you couldn't remember what the title of the movie was. It's called '*Proof*'."

She stopped me again, "Hey, I don't know what you are taking about. I did not talk to you yesterday and have not talked with you in a couple of weeks. And what are you going on about with this movie? I was in a coffee shop with a co-worker for most of the day yesterday and we were doing something especially important. I don't even think I had my phone on."

I was so confused! My head was spinning. I recovered quickly stating that I mixed her up with her Aunt Mo, knowing that was not the case. I can assure you, my daughter would in no way play a prank on me like this especially knowing I was into the Mandela Effect, without eventually coming clean, at the very least. And to further the story. I heard about it from a few other family members about what I should and should not be talking about to people. Yes, I got the calls. You either have the patience to be ridiculed at every turn or you do not.

Present day: I had not discussed this event with my daughter since it happened. I recently spoke with her and we were talking about Mandela Effects. The Monopoly man wears a monocle, Curious George has a tail, Mickey Mouse wears suspenders and the Statue of Liberty is on Ellis Island. All of her answers were how I remembered them, and as most of you know, all of those answers are wrong. She stated that when I first started talking about the changes, she really was not paying attention. She was busy with physical reality and kind of blew it off, again thinking it was something weird I was into. But, since then she has heard of the term Mandela Effect from a number of people, and she feels like she kind of knew a little more about it. After I described the above story to her, she was amazed. She started out by stating she would not have known who Louis Anderson was, she never heard of him. Family Feud was not one of her normal shows, if at all. She stated that she was in New York around that time and that she only recalls one time that she was in a coffee shop doing a project with a girlfriend, but not a Starbucks.

Also, during this conversation, I brought up things like waking at 9am, going back to sleep and waking again at 8am. I brought up Mohammad Ali dying once and then dying again and that Gene Wilder dies every ten years for me. Also, Nichelle Nicolas and how she died twice for me, obviously in different timelines, because she is still alive today. With that, I reminded her of something strange that happened to her. At the end of January, she noticed a post from her girlfriend stating that she just found out that she was pregnant, picture and all. And a couple of days ago the post came up again, for the very first time. Her girlfriend announced that she just found out that she was pregnant. The shame of it was, she had to go as she was pressed for time, and we were having a great conversation about this stuff. One like I would have never expected. She has been so busy, I mean distracted, with physical things like school and a boyfriend, friends and family and of course work and bills, that there was no way she had time to concern herself with changes in history or Shifting Timelines, Realities, Dimensions or what have you. In terms I like to use, having her accept the idea that physical reality is different in some way, sprung her Dominate Consciousness to a closer Timeline to where my Dominate Consciousness resides. Nice feeling. And I suspect, this will be happening with many people soon. I do feel that the truth will be seen by all. How will that pan out? I cannot say, but something tells me there will be many decisions to be made by many people.

Was it the same day that I watched *'Proof'*? I do not recall. I would assume I had enough of movies for one day, after all of that. Yet, I know it was not too long after watching *"Proof"* that I popped in *'Batman Begins'*. Already having the experience with knowing the dialogue of a movie that I have never seen, and coincidently, and no, I do not believe in coincidences, picking out a movie that was only described to me, apparently from an aspect of my daughter from another timeline, you would think that I would take another experience with a calm demeanor and just experience the phenomenon and observe. Well, this experience was a bit on the creepy side.

I have seen *'Batman Begins'* multiple times. This dialogue I know. About a half of an hour into the movie, *Christian Bale*, the lead actor in the movie, is staring directly at me while he is saying his lines. I refocused my eyes assuming the scene would look normal after I cleared them. Nothing changed, except that it felt like I was getting a message from the actor. I had no time to contemplate this as I was fairly distraught. Hiding behind a pillow, I reached for the remote and struck pause.

This experience was unnerving, to say the least. Thinking back on the event, it was the same, in that the air or atmosphere seemed thicker. But this idea did not stem from the experience, it came from looking back. What I mean to express, is that when I feel a shift is taking place or when I am shifting into another adjacent Timeline, I do not know it at the time of the experience. Yet, I feel like I could if I paid a bit more attention.

I plucked up the nerve to watch some more of the movie. The only difference was I was looking for a message. I was on alert. Nothing came. Until my focus came off of looking for something and went back to the movie. Two more characters started staring at me, but this time I did get a message, or more accurately, a feeling that they were asking me a question. I kept getting in my head, *"What are you waiting for?"*

This stopped me in my tracks. I did not finish the movie that evening. I went off to contemplate my latest experience and wrote it down.

The movie *'Proof'* was the most exceptional experience I had with the movies. But they all could be categorized as supernatural or paranormal. *'Prometheus'* was no different in that I was amazed at what was taking place. This is a movie that I had wanted to see since it came out and I just never got to it. The release date was 2001. This was taking place in 2016. I remember thinking it was odd that the movie had already been out for ten years. So, wait a minute. The math does not add up. And it even gets stranger as the actual release date is 2012. There have been other Mandela Effect movie release date changes. People have reported already seeing movies that have not been released. A mother and daughter have posted that after seeing the '*Disney*' movie '*Aladdin*', when it first came out, they ran out to get the soundtrack as there was a song they really enjoyed in the movie. The song was not on the soundtrack. So, the next day they went to the movies to see '*Aladdin*' again and the song they were looking for was nowhere to be found.

Besides the discrepancy with the release dates on the '*Prometheus*' movie, there was also the experience of me knowing the entire dialogue of this movie. Maybe not the actual words but the story line for sure. I know I have never seen this movie! I almost bought the DVD in stores many times and always figured I would catch it somewhere else at another time. All but the end of the movie was exactly how I knew it would play out. As I contemplated this, I started to have a memory of watching this movie from my phone. This did not make sense to me as I rarely watched anything on my phone and would have only recently learned I could get Netflix on my phone. There came a time when I stopped watching anything on media. And that was just after the impalement. I definitely could find other things to distract myself. And distracting myself was the last thing on my mind. I do not recall ever watching 'Prometheus' prior to moving to Mississippi. Yet, there is a memory of it? The desire to see this movie, that I have never seen, is much stronger than the idea of a memory of me watching the movie.

CONSCIOUSNESS SHIFT

It seemed that each time I had a question, the answer would be given to me in the form of some weird, strange paranormal or supernatural involvement. I wanted to understand the moon, sun and stars, when the stars gave me their show. I was exploring the idea of different dimensions when I walked into the cigar shop. And now, my question was when we shift, if we do indeed shift our consciousness, do we keep the same body? Well, if we are shifting every nano-second than we are never in the same body, but my answer came by means of a physical change on my body.

Back in 2015 and 2016, even though I was having all of these incredible experiences and I was and still am very against watching television as a distraction, I needed to slow down. I would actually make a point to take some time out to watch some episode on Netflix. Not surprisingly my focus was on two shows, *Fringe* and *Continuum*. One afternoon, I was watching a *Fringe* episode where Peter Bishop was showing a child a G.I. Joe figurine. He looked at the figurine and stated that he always remembered a specific scar on the other side of the toy. I did not think much of that until I was browsing through the Mandela Effect web site and someone mentioned that the date tattooed on their bodies changed dates. The date was her birthday and her mother's death. Her and her friends all had the date tattooed on their bodies. Other people started chiming in on the thread stating that they also had tattoo's change as well as scars changing from one side of their body to the other. I thought this interesting as I had a distinctive scar under my left elbow.

I was in my early twenties when I walked into the Medical One Emergency Room. I had a gash under my left elbow from an acquaintance who rubbed my arm in broken glass. The doctor and two nurses just stared at the meat hanging off of my arm. The doctor looked at me and stated that he could do one of two things. He could take off all of the skin around the area and hope it heals well. Or he could do an experimental stitch. I said, "Doc, it's my left arm and I am right-handed. It is also under my elbow. I am not worried about any scar, if you want to do an experimental stitch, by all means, go right ahead." He did his experimental stitch and it left an interesting distinctive 'C' scar under my left elbow.

This is something specific I would not forget. The scar being under my left elbow is significant as when I went to check on it after reading all of the comments about tattoos and scars changing, I was amazed to see that it completely healed. Then I glanced over under my right elbow and there it was. The perfect 'C' scar exactly the opposite way it was on my left arm. I stood and stared. Then, in a split second my mind tried to justify it. I have been through this already, so I intentionally stopped. I decided to accept it. It did not take too long for me to realize that this was an answer to my question.

No, we do not continuously keep the same physical body. It seems to me, that the only thing that is real is the consciousness and that is all that is shifting and all that we are experiencing. Yet, do our memories shift? I have assumed that whatever your dominate consciousness is experiencing will be your memories. But this seems to be untrue. An example would be the 'Prometheus' movie where I feel I may have seen the movie in another Timeline, and shifted into that Timeline, having me feel as if I had already seen the movie. Now, I did not have a memory of seeing the movie, but I did recall over ninety percent of it. So, it seems I shifted into a Timeline where the memories from that movie were still intact.

I started to create my own YouTube videos. I wanted to understand what the hell was going on. And the best way for me to do this was to create these videos for myself, to see if I could figure out what was happening. Of course, there was also the idea that someone else may have had similar experiences and I could research from there or learn or help.

The first three or four videos I released; I state that the Earth is flat. Looking back this bothered me now because I clearly recall pushing towards life being about your perception and not about something that is so far removed, you can't physically interact with it or prove it. By the time I made my fifth video I was stating that life is about your perception. That it did not matter if the Earth were a ball, flat as a pancake or a triangle. It was quickly becoming about me, or rather each individual, and what I/we perceive and how we interact with the people around us.

After I created about one hundred and fifty videos, I started to look back at the first few videos I created. I swear it was not me. Or what I should say is, it did not look like the way I remember looking. I was heavier by a lot more than I recall. My inflections were off a bit and other thing just didn't seem right. Now, after the explanation on how we shift and what we shift it is obvious that it was not my original body. Basically, I shifted to a Timeline where I was actually that heavy and so on.

FRIENDS, FAMILY & PROXIMITY

Friends and family. What can I say? I am sure anyone who is experiencing the Mandela Effect is having difficulty dealing with family members. You may have been the one in the family always looking for the conspiracy and maybe even finding it. That is the way it was for me. So, at first, I was just blown off by most of my family when I spoke about stars shooting out at me or orbs telling me not to eat meat. The surprising thing to me was that two of my closest friends were not interested at all when I first mentioned my experiences. This was bizarre since both of them would normally have jumped at the chance to explore a fresh conspiracy or a new supernatural phenomenon. Now I find myself wondering if I was not in some other Timeline when I spoke with them. Because now, they get it. One is aware of the shifts yet moves about his day normally dealing with a job and family. The other is too wrapped up in a career and family and really does not have the time. I get it, believe me I do.

Most people just blow off the information and return to their routine. I cannot blame them, I mean physical reality is nothing like you have been taught, told or programmed to believe. Or it was linear and solid and now it's not, it's changed. Either way, what does somebody do with that mind chaos? Once in a while I would come across someone who would really listen, and that is when everything would change. I found myself talking to many people about the experiences I had. With the people I did not know personally, like my roommates and co-workers, I was simply being appeased by them. Even little things are hard to bring up. And this brings me to what is referred to as Flip-Flops in the Mandela Effect community.

When I was visiting family, back on the east coast, I noticed that '*Tidy Cats*', which is what I have always known it to be spelled, was now '*Tidy Cat*'. I mentioned this to a few people, and they all blew it off as if they misremembered, like it was always '*Tidy Cat*'. This upset me some, but at that time I was tired of chasing Mandela Effects. I simply laughed and shelved it in the back of my mind.

Sometime later, I decided to adopt a couple of cats and name them after Mandela Effects. At the time, I was not in a position to own two cats, I just knew, owning cats was something I wanted to do. Strangely enough, the change happened long before I bought the cats. When I mentally decided to adopt two cats is when I noticed the brand '*Tidy Cats*' was back, as I remembered it before. I ended up getting Buttercup and Prince just over a year later. Like I inferred earlier, after a while you just become numb and except the fact that physical reality changes and shifts.

Once, I was sitting at a bar in Mississippi and talking with the barmaid about the Mandela Effect. I gave her a quiz. She passed for the most part, meaning she answered most of the questions the way they were then in that Timeline. But it was when I asked about '*Sex and the City*' that her life changed. I felt she might have shifted right then and there. She started telling me that she watches the show every night and even gets it on her phone and that it is one hundred percent titled '*Sex in The City*'. I told her to look it up. I knew exactly when it happened. The look on her face was one of such bewilderment, I felt horrible for guiding her to see truth or whatever it is some of us are seeing. I know she looked into it a bit further and then just did not have the time. What happened? Either she shifted her dominate consciousness to where she didn't have to deal with such paranormal supernatural nonsense or she stayed in this Timeline where she just justified whatever she could to keep her mind sane, and keep her daily routine.

And when it came to talking with friends and family back east over the phone, it was like they were at my funeral. Some of them sounded as if they were saying the eulogy. "I am glad you're happy and at peace", one said. My ex-girlfriend was saying things like, "It was wonderful having you in my life then and now". Another, exclaimed, "Oh, you're still alive." Even though I consciously noticed this while it was happening, I threw it on the back burner. Not because I thought I would actually contemplate and compare what people were saying but because I was just too overwhelmed at the time to take any of what others were saying to me seriously. I really do not think they believed me when I explained these experiences. Although, the ex-girlfriend was affected and interested in the experiences I shared, she was and is too wrapped up in her physical life with her husband and children. How am I supposed to explain to her that they are having the life they need to experience, in some other reality?

After a couple of months, I started talking with my sister a lot. She was there for me while I was going through some tough times in Mississippi. We spoke of Flat Earth theories and of course the Mandela Effects along with some of the other things that were going on with me. I suspected right from the beginning that I was being watched by my family. But if that was the case, it did not stay that way. When I first called her, I started the conversation with a Mandela Effect I am sure she was familiar with and would have an answer for. She is a deeply religious person, so information on the bible should be easy to find. I asked her what animal lied down with the lamb? My sister draws quite often and is quite good. She laughed out loud explaining that she was painting a picture of the lion and lamb, as we spoke. I do not recall her exact response to it actually being the wolf and the lamb, but I do recall denial. I decided to go a little further down the rabbit hole with her. I was explaining the orb experience, then the star experience. After explaining the star experience, she said immediately, "Maybe you were having a heart attack?" This sentence caught my attention. Why not? If death is a catalyst for shifting your consciousness from one Timeline to another, I suppose this could have been the case. Yet, it is much more exciting to think that the stars were communicating with me, and that the veil was lifted, and I was seeing truth.

While I was in Mississippi, she and I would talk almost every day. She was following everything I was saying about perception and the theories I was entertaining. And she was affected by the Mandela Effect. After I moved away from Mississippi and back to Colorado, we did not talk as much. The one-hour time difference was apparently too much. My work hours changed as well. Now, with the lack of focus on Mandela Effects and my other experiences, she focused elsewhere, and it seemed at the time that we slipped into different Timelines. About a year later, she is not interested in these paranormal supernatural experiences that we discussed. Not at all, at least at that time. On top of that she began telling me about the kittens she acquired some months earlier and apparently, she thought I knew what she was talking about. I had no idea what she was going on about a certain cat that she told me about before. I just answered as if I knew what was going on. I had no patience to explain that my consciousness was not in this Timeline when she gathered these kittens. Now, I suspect another Shift occurred as her and my mother joke about shifting into other timelines when they notice something is different, whether it is a Mandela Effect or not.

I have family members I consider myself close to, even though I may only speak with them once a year. I never found that strange. But now I think, wow, what if they live somewhere in another Timeline nowhere near my Dominate Consciousness. Granted this was just a dream, yet one of those vivid like dreams, where my brother fell from atop a spiral staircase and perished. I rewound the scene and changed the outcome of the dream. I surmised that in some other reality or dimension he may have perished, yet my Dominate Consciousness did not have to go through the pain and suffering of living a life without him in it. So, unconsciously, from a 3D physical standpoint, I Shifted into a Timeline where

I did not have to go through that pain. But who or what finalized that decision? It had to be some form of me, right? When you get down to it, you are the only one really involved. What I mean to say is with infinite timelines, no one should be in the same dimension, density or realm. Consider the terms I use. They could be interchangeable, which does not make things any easier to explain.

This may get a bit twisted here, but I think this audience will understand this theory.

We are all in our own dimension. We interact with one another on a daily basis easily since we reside in a Timeline within the same parameters. We are able to do this because our Dominate Consciousness's are on the same Main Timeline. The more distant you are with someone, the further removed their dominate consciousness will be to yours, yet we still get to interact with them. We are living in a multidimensional reality, not necessarily just a physical one. I read or saw a video somewhere, where a woman said her father always used to say something like, 'you can't kill me, I am the star of this show.' What if our consciousness is the only consciousness in a specific dimension? I am sure paths will cross, but even when they do, it would most likely only be for a nano-second. If you are the only one in a specific Dimension, then nothing matters except your Consciousness and the experience. Yet, we are all still in a vibrational Timeline as a Collective. So, it is not solipsism. I know it sounds a bit like solipsism, and it just might be close, but it is also about the way you interact with others. For you, from your perspective, it is not about them, but the way you respond to them. And the same goes for each and every one of us. This makes us the Collective. So, as much as you may be the only awareness in a specific dimension or density, this is no time to be selfish. We are all in this together. And we are moving through time as a Collective, well, at least from the Collective's perspective. I know I am repeating myself, but this is pretty deep. Even though I say we are in different Dimensions, we are still within the same vibrational Timeline within certain parameters, which makes it is easy to interact with one another.

Ever wonder why one friend or other breaks ties with you? Ever wonder why that lover just up and left? One of your consciousness's shifted away from the other. Yes, it could have been you, even if you did not think you wanted that to happen. How is that? Because we have all been programmed to not use our feelings and emotions. Feelings and emotions are a key ingredient for creating the physical life you want to live.

Another thing that seemed to be happening to me during these many months of experiences, was that I felt as if I was being cleansed. I do not know how else to explain it and I wasn't doing it consciously. I was clearing out a lot of negative and old feelings that I gathered throughout my life. I found myself forgiving people I forgot about for circumstances that I thought were concluded. Something would happen and it would trigger a memory. It could have been something as simple as my roommate walking in the door.

Once, while in Mississippi, I had a very strange occurrence that shook me. It was not like I wasn't used to strange things happening to me, it was that each time a new experience happened I would examine it differently or more closely. No experience was the same. One morning I woke in a sweat screaming 'DE85930, DE85930" repeatedly until I was completely awake. It sounded so familiar to me. I knew these letters and numbers, but I couldn't figure out what they were. I wrote them down, even though I was sure I would not forget them. I am not sure how long it took me to figure out what they were but when I did, it was numbing.

Sometime in 1985, I decided to give my high school sweetheart a call to say hello. This is some five years later. For the life of me, I could not recall her phone number. In the nineties before I was to be married, I tried again to contact her and say hello. I called old friends and looked up what I could, to no avail. In 2000 and 2006 I tried again. It was harmless enough, I just felt the need to say hello, each of these times. Well, apparently, I had some unfinished business with this girl. To this day I don't know exactly what it was that was going on but when I discovered that I woke screaming out her old phone number some thirty-five years later, I thought it might be important to contact her. At first the letters in the beginning threw me off, but back then is when phone numbers began with letters. Of course, after thirty-five years the number did not work, and I was still unable to contact her. So, I laid down and meditated on her. I do not recall the entire meditation, but I do recall me imagining having a conversation with her and I came out of the meditation with a wet face feeling refreshed and revived. It was like I was given back a part of my soul.

I only spent six months in Mississippi, working in a casino. The area is not for everyone. I knew I wanted to leave, and I was not even sure where I would go. I just knew I needed to leave. I was frustrated at the time thinking I could be stuck in Mississippi for a couple of years. I wanted answers and I wanted them now. I happened to come across information on automatic writing. I thought, "why not?" Let me give it a try. I did not know what I was doing and did not know what to expect. I took the book I was keeping notes in and posed an obscure question, by writing the question down in the book. The answer came as fast as the question. I do not know how to explain this but as soon as I finished writing the question mark, I started writing the answer. A couple more questions, all based on where I was living and my career, flew out of my pen. The answers came just as easily. It was the final answer that I could not believe would happen. I asked when I would be out of Mississippi. And I also asked when I would be back in Colorado. The answer to both questions, was April. Now if the answer would have come back as May or the end of the year, I would have understood that, but it did not, it came back as April. I thought, that would be great! I just did not understand how that was possible with other projects and such having to be taken care of. May or June would have made much more sense. Yet no sooner did April come around and I found myself in a position where I could easily leave my job and comfortably go anywhere I wanted. All these things I feel I created. I needed to cleanse, whether I knew it or not. The emotion was present, and the desire was connected, to being able to create. Meaning, cleansing or being cleansed, is probably a prerequisite to creating.

CATALYSTS AND TRIGGERS

Assuming these theories and hypotheses are accurate or even close to true, then we can feel confident that death is not real. We don't die, we just shift our consciousness to an adjoining parallel Timeline and continue on with our life as if nothing happened. There are more than likely a number of other things involved, which I have not speculated on. The idea that it was dark and that I did not see what was going on could be a major factor. I did not have to believe it. But what does that mean if the only thing one might have to get used to would be a line changing in a song?

When someone dies in your life, they die for you. They die so you can experience life without them physically. Their consciousness moves on to another parallel Timeline where they are still interacting with you. Now, from their perspective, you both may have become distant because where your Dominate Consciousness resides, they are dead.

This can get a bit intricate. And that is why I say, "it is about you'. I do not intend to get into solipsism again, but it seems to fit, even if a bit off. You are the only one aware of your consciousness. You have no idea what is going on in anyone else's mind. If you are in a family or relationship where the people around you are like robots or I should say where it is like you are nothing more than an observer, than you may have died in the dominate consciousness's of all of those people. If this seems to be the case, I advise walking around happy. Let them know you are simply great with everything. I tried this and from my experience, I have noticed a change with family members. They were never as distant as they are now and not just because of the physical distance. I was the one who moved away. And I am usually the one who will make the phone call. I still talk with all of them here and there and there are no worries from any angle. When someone passes in your life, all you want to know is that they are not in any pain and that they are happy. So, show all of those who are not near your dominate consciousness that you are just fine! This allows them to get on with their lives as well as you with yours. Even if people are not dominantly conscious in the Timeline you reside in, they will still receive incite and information from you, even if just in a dream.

One experience I had after returning to Colorado was finding out that something in the bible, that I am very familiar with, was different. *'The Lord's Prayer'*, or is it called *'The Our Father'*? Anyway, I recall the line being '*On* Earth as it is in Heaven' not '*In* Earth as it is in Heaven' which, apparently is what it has always been. Also, the word, 'debts', was not in the lines when I first had to memorize it. At this time, I was already aware of the Lion and Wolf switch, dwelling with the lamb, but the real surprise for me was when I found out that there was a raven and a dove that went off to find land for Noah and his ark. And let us not forget that Unicorns are now in the bible. Although I am not a bible thumper by any means and have no right to claim that I know what is in the bible or what is not in the bible. This would be a good place to write my favorite bible verse, as it has not changed, as of this printing. (Printed in Red) ~**"Verily, verily, I say unto you, He that believeth on me, the works that I do shall he do also; and greater works than these shall he do; because I go unto my Father."** ~

Well, this possible Mandela Effect is interesting. I could only go to my immediate family with this one, as that is where my trigger was. I recall without a shadow of a doubt, that in Catholic bibles, and I found out later in a few other denominations as well, that when Jesus spoke, the print in the bible was always in red. I remember this in class as I went to a Catholic school. I remember teachers mentioning this as well, but it was my family that would confirm my suspicions that this was not the case any longer. I called up three relatives and asked about the words of Jesus being written in red. None of them knew what I was talking about. One said they remembered seeing red highlights in a bible before, thinking they could have been Jesus' words, but they were not sure. These people, or should I say the dominate consciousness' of these family members probably reside in a Timeline where I have died. This possibly occurred around the time of the impalement or earlier when I was watching volcano videos. If nothing else, they act very differently from the way I remember them acting. Oh, sure people change, but not that drastically, overnight.

I know this can be a touchy subject. One that I have had with a few people. There was a girl at the bar I work in that I spoke with about my impalement experience. She had a look of shock in her eyes as I spoke. She started to get terribly upset, so I stopped talking, calmed her down and asked her to explain why she was so upset. She began to tell me that she tried to kill herself five days in a row. A bottle of pills one day, pills with alcohol the next day. She woke up both days completely confused about why she was still alive. She explained how bad things were for her back then and continued telling me about the next three days, bleeding out for two days and the last with her jumping off of the top of a barn into barbed wire and standing up with nothing but a scratch. I am not saying you cannot kill yourself; I do not know. What I am saying is that for some people, depending on where they are in their evolution as a human being, may not be able to take their own life. We may just shift to an adjacent Timeline. What would be the point of trying to take your life anyway if you keep coming back to finish whatever it is that you are here to finish. I feel that what may happen when you actually die, and that would mean you strongly believe you can only live to be very old at best, is that your consciousness transfers to a baby avatar and you start over again. As in reincarnation, but I think it is different than the known definition. I feel that much of what has been taught from a spiritual viewpoint is incomplete or doctored to feed another agenda. It seems that anything that was created by the system we live in, is a lie. Or, as in the case with my impalement, you stay on that specific main Timeline theme and you just revert to a Timeline where you did not die.

The phrase, 'Main Timeline Theme' that I am using portrays a Main Timeline, where most of the things you experience are incased within. Within this main Timeline there are many more that branch off, but the main theme or the parameters stays the same. When one shifts and notices a large change in something, it can be said that they shifted to an external, distant or foreign Timeline. Picture a handful of straws and wrap those straws in a rubber band. The rubber band is a dimension with specific parameters and all of the straws are and become an infinite number of similar Timelines. Now picture many rubber bands encasing many straws. These are all separate Physical Dimensions that we can apparently shift our consciousness to. Can we have and experience whatever we want? The time is right, and we are experiencing the idea of instant manifestation through the idea of shifting our consciousness through Timelines. Why not? This may be why I and others in my town are walking around scratching our heads wondering if we had died. The transfer of consciousness is now nearly instant. And how would you know? Because now, as an example, the *Monopoly Man* has never worn a monocle in this Timeline, when you are sure he had.

Most of the people I run into or talk to about these things have a death story or a story that brought them close to death. I do not mean out of body experiences. I mean something like, they were in an accident and they do not understand how they were fine a few days later. Or the story I read on-line about how one man spoke about being in an accident totaling his car and woke up the next day in his bed and his car was in the driveway and not totaled.

Let me digress and explain further the ideas and theories that coincide with me watching the volcano videos in February of 2015. I remembered looking at quite a few volcano videos a day, on the volcanos and how they could erupt any day. I went looking for these videos months after I initially watched them. I surmised that the idea of a mass death causing a mass amount of people to experience the Mandela Effect could be plausible. I went back almost two years in my history. Further than I needed to go. There was not one volcano video in my history. What could that have meant? Did a volcano erupt killing thousands or millions, having all of them shift their consciousness to an adjacent Timeline where the volcanos did not erupt? If everything holds true, I will assume that there would be mass shifts.

And death may not be the only catalyst for shifting. There are also trigger dates that have been noticed by me and others. Every year around September 23rd especially, but it also seems like the month of May is also some sort of trigger date. I say this because that is when some of the largest Mandela Effects have shown up as well as other events, which seem to take place during those times.

There have also been a few formulas I have come across that supposedly help you shift. I would suggest making sure you are in a great state of mind, when trying anything you read about. The idea here is that, like attracts like and you will shift yourself into a Timeline which best lines up with your present attitude, demeanor, emotions etc.

I found one formula that seemed harmless. This is to be done between midnight and three in the morning. I took a candle and lit it in the bathroom. I stood with the candle in-between me and the mirror, and I stared at myself in the mirror for a good twenty minutes. The experiences of what I saw, could have been very frightening except that, at this point, I was deep into weird events taking place. I started to get bold and experiment. I figured there was nothing to fear. Most of the time I would notice my face shaking in the mirror. Twice it went from the right side of the mirror to the other, as I stood right in the middle. I also started to see other faces in the mirror. Did I shift my consciousness from one Timeline to another? Maybe. It was an exhilarating experience and one that helped me out of the funk of being skittish about every little thing. I was becoming the scientist now, experimenting without fear, and going as far as I could go and then I would go a bit further.

I also feel that one can purposefully shift their consciousness to a Timeline more to their liking. Even if just for one specific event or idea. I have experimented with the weather. I successfully shifted my consciousness into a Timeline where the weather did not impede my plans. Did I do this? I consciously spoke saying the snow will miss this town. And it did. Every city around me had six inches or more of snow. We had nothing. I went away for three days, leaving the area with no weather problems. When I returned, I just laughed. The second I parked my car in front of my residence, it began to snow and there was six inches of the white stuff staring at me for an entire week. I have experimented further with these ideas and have been mostly successful. I do not totally understand what I am supposed to do all the time, because you have to just do it. And one of the ingredients, is to not talk about it, so …

Were there consequences to my actions? If in fact I did shift my consciousness to another adjacent timeline, the only consequence I specifically recall would be getting used to the new lyrics in one of *Prince's* songs. *"Dearly beloved, we are gathered here today to 'celebrate' this thing called life"*, changed to *"Dearly beloved we are gathered here today to 'get through' this thing called life".* Although, with what I have actually created for myself in the past few months, the only thing that I may have had to get used to was Kit-Kat not having the dash or some other product change or pop-culture difference, the shift wasn't that drastic. I contend that we can in fact, jump to a Timeline far removed from where our dominate consciousness resides, and have drastic changes.

If there is one thing, I would like for you to understand, it is that these things aren't changing. The song lyrics did not change, you did! Nothing is changing, except for your consciousness and perspective. The lyrics in this song have always been *'to get through this thing called life',* in this Timeline. No one is wrong. You may remember *'celebrate'* and your friends may not. It would depend on where their dominate consciousness resided when they heard the song.

Because of my experiences, and the interpretations of my questions and answers, I have come to the conclusion that for me, I am to help and either find a way to break out of the physical realm, which some might call the matrix, or continue on creating my reality through my perception by shifting my consciousness through Timelines. The latter makes more sense. And it may just be that the only way to break free from this physical realm; if in fact that is what one might want to accomplish. Knowing that physical reality is malleable, knowing you can create by shifting into that which already is, would eventually have you create a way to leave this realm, when ready. Would it not?

If your reality is based on your perception, which I feel to be accurate. Then, it is only a matter of your focus. I have heard theories that those who follow Jesus and await him to bring them into paradise, experience just that. Those who think that there is no spirit or soul and just fade to dust will experience nothingness, be it only for a time. If you focus on shifting your consciousness into a Timeline where it is a natural thing to shift and have all kinds of supernatural experiences, it seems to me that, that is what you will experience.

What is the one thing we all really want to know? We want to know what it is, to be who we really are. We want to know what it was like before we got here. Do we really know? No, we do not. Most of the people I have come in contact within my life seem to believe we have a spirit. I would correct them by stating we do not have a spirit, but that we are a spirit experiencing a physical illusion. And again, then there is the possibility that we are a spirit experiencing this reality through a computer program. Which might make one feel confined. That could be the reason for the deception of the shape of the Realm we reside on or in. If we believe there is an infinite number of planets out in space then, as humans, we do not feel confined or trapped. But, if we knew we were in a Realm where there was boundaries and not outer space, that this is the only physical dimension, then we would feel confined and some would stop at nothing to break free. If it is a Realm and this is the only physical reality, whether a computer program or an illusion by some other design, then maybe we all are stuck in this trap. But are we stuck? Or is it that we are experiencing something that was impossible to experience in the first place. Should we not be creating?

Everything already is. Consciousness in the moment is all that you are experiencing. Wherever your energy vibrational level stands, that is what your consciousness will experience. Tune your vibration to what you desire and shift your consciousness to that Timeline where you are filled with the desire to create. Your desire must be in line with your heart's desire. The desires of the mind have been polluted since the day of your birth. This really began when your personality was formed by your peers, teachers, parent's authority and society in general that is what I have found while doing my own experiments. My desires were not in line with my true desires. Once they are in line, realize that what you are creating already exists. Feel the presence of the desire in action. Know it is alive and real. See it, feel it. Verbally decree it a thing and it shall be. Voice out loud the desire you know to be and be confident when you see the desire unfold. Finally, surrender to what you know already exists and all will be exposed in Divine Time. And do not speak of it. You are just shifting your consciousness to the Timeline where your desire is already alive and thriving.

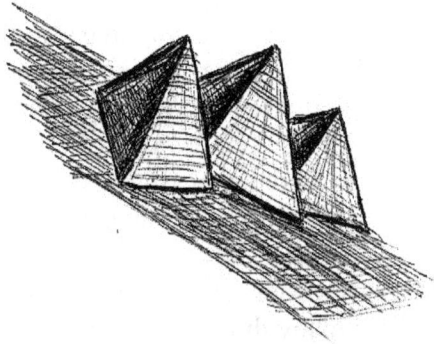

THE OUTWARD CONNECTION

You will not see a direct mention of the Mandela Effect on the evening news. If it is, it will let you know people are just misremembering things and be a subtle hint in a commercial which is more than likely poking fun at the Mandela Effect affected. This will most likely stay on the internet, which could be the sheep telling the wolf everything. I have also advised many times to not watch television or give your energy and power away to the news and other media outlets. It is my understanding that spectator sports and video games are just as poisoning as the news, which pulls your emotions in all directions, North, East, West, and South. This keeps your emotions in check, and you cannot use your emotions to create properly because your head and your heart are not lined up. You know your heart is lined up. You are just not used to communicating with your heart in that way. Practice, it's a very exciting way to experience life.

After a year of experiencing Mandela Effects, other supernatural experiences and talking with others who also had experiences, I decided to post a video on YouTube about some of the things that were happening to me. At the time, I was very sure the earth was not a globe. Yet, I was saying the Earth was flat, when in fact I did not know. This could have been my biggest mistake, as I have already taken the word of authority about many things that just are not true or known at all. If nothing else, it was proven to me that there was something very suspicious about the moon landing. Or is that landings? It depends (or is that *Depend*), on which Timeline you resided in, at the time. Yes, the number of moon landings has changed and is listed as a Mandela Effect.

I made my way back into Colorado in April of 2016. Not long after returning, I thought I would take a break from Mandela Effects. (I wasn't going back to the ball, that is too depressing.) But the moment I turned my back on them, the largest Mandela Effect hit me like a ton of bricks.

No, it was not the pyramids, although I have noticed they have changed as well. It was the J.F.K. assassination. I studied the J.F.K. assassination at great length with other friends back in 1985. This memory is strong for me and is a trigger point. The car was occupied by William Greer, the driver; Texas Governor, John Connally in the passenger seat; First Lady Jackie Kennedy, sitting behind the driver and J.F.K. sitting on the right side of his wife. There were four people in that car and now I find out there was actually six? Besides that, the car is different, and the angle of the camera is a bit off, among other things. This brought me right back to exploring Mandela Effects, although my stance was to stop chasing them.

One year into doing Mandela Effect videos, I started to go back and watch the first few videos I published. Watching the first video, I did not recognize myself. Not only that, the message was off from what I recall saying. It was still intact but the whole reason I went out to the Gulf of Mexico the next day was to do another video because I felt that I had left out an especially important idea. The idea was about perception and how it does not matter what shape the planet is. It is about what is around you and how you interact with it. Now, this idea does not show up until about the fifth video. It does seem that when you shift, you can change your past.

By my third or fifth video I was stating that we do not know if the Earth is flat but because of the experience I had with the stars, I will say that the stars are not suns with planets revolving around them. With that, the truest statement I can make is that I feel that we do not live on a spinning ball flying at incredible speeds through the vacuum of space. This idea seems so prosperous to me now. The Earth may very well be flat. In my opinion it is probably malleable and is more like a Realm. But the truth is, I just do not know. The biggest problem I see with the flat Earth awakening, if I can call it that, is that we all have been programmed and indoctrinated into the globe from birth. As a baby, one might play with the planets hanging over the crib. As a small child one would see the globe upon walking into a classroom. And by the time we are teenagers there would be no reason to question the authority about living on a globe spinning through space. The notion of anything else would seem ridiculous. Anyone claiming that the earth was flat will be looked at like a complete crackpot. Society and the media have taken care of that since before the nineteen-hundreds. There is a lot of information on what the planet may or may not be. Explore and investigate but be cautious of homing in on one absolute definitive answer. Because no one, really knows.

After about ten videos, I started really zeroing in on the Mandela Effect and leaving the flat earth information alone. I did not really care. I mean, I get why we should be upset that we were lied to forever about the blue marble theory, but life is about your perception and you cannot see the edge, so it is not in your perception, so it does not have to be a part of your life. Like the news and wars. Oh, and I can hear someone saying, 'well it's good to be informed on what is going on in the world'. Be informed. But know, it is not real, it is all an act and you are falling into a trap. In a few of my videos, I say stop watching the news, that the news is not important, unless you put it in your perception. They are just sucking up your energy. Well, in most cases that is probably true. But should one not be aware of what is going on in the world? I say be informed if you feel you need to be informed, but do not get wrapped up in the drama. It is really up to the individual on how far they want to take the information. As it would be up to the individual on how far down the rabbit hole, they wanted to go. As it will be for the individual to decide where to put their focus and what they want to experience in this illusionary physical Realm.

If you do not know about people killing other people for whatever reason it cannot bother you, but it does affect you. And now some say, but I need to know, what if they come near my home and my family. I say, where is your focus? All you are doing is drumming up fear and creating that reality. Stop! And, if you are sitting on the couch watching CNN and the war, well you are drumming up emotions that you dislike, because they will make you physically sick and will eventually make you suppress these emotions. And emotions are one of the main keys to creating your reality. Watching spectator sports or movies on Netflix, Hulu or other media outlets is just as negative as watching live television. So, do you see by watching television you are giving your power away and this not the direction humanity wants to be going in? If they only knew. Find something new and creative to entertain yourself with. Do something with your hands and make it about you. Do something physical. Write! Draw! If humans, as a Collective, continue to give their power away, the elite will soon have their world war or their cyborg race or wherever it is you are focusing your energy on. And in one Timeline or another they have just that. Why would you want your consciousness to reside there? Do you really need to experience that?

I really started to enjoy doing videos and posting them. After the first year, I felt that I was doing the right thing by telling the stories about my experiences. My first reason for posting these videos was twofold. First and foremost, I was posting for me. I wanted to listen to myself and maybe figure something out while listening to myself talk. Second maybe someone else has had an experience and they could either help me figure some things out or maybe my video could help them. Now I can honestly say I enjoy making these videos and I can be honest and say that is all ego. I can associate with my ego now without letting it control me. I know it is not about me as much as it is about what I do and how I respond. It is true, that you are the only one in your head and you are the only consciousness in a Timeline, Density or Dimension at any given time, but always remember you are not in this alone. This is a collective and we need each other.

One and a half years later, after posting my first YouTube video I have over one hundred and fifty videos posted. My very first video I came out firing. I explained the experience of the stars communicating with me. I am not sure that was the way to go, but it worked out, nonetheless. I do claim the Earth may be flat in my first few videos, but I convalesce quickly realizing that I have no idea what the shape of the Earth is. I just do not know. I do know I have been lied to and mislead. Either way I was deceived. The first one hundred videos or so are an average of seven minutes long and give my thoughts on many ideas from consciousness to outer space. The last fifty or so really get down to the meat of things. These are the videos that I enjoyed the most as I learned the most.

I did a few videos in 2017, where I am interviewing people at the bar I work in, asking them, "What color is a Yield sign?" The answer I mostly got was that it was yellow. No, it has not been yellow since 1972 and I have read somewhere that it was never yellow in the United States, although that information cannot be found, at this time. And to expand on that, I would ask what shape the Yield sign is and most of the time, if not all the time, the response, was always an upside-down triangle. So, I've seen the yellow to red difference and I also noticed the shape difference, because the shape was a diamond, not a triangle. Well, it seems I am wrong or more accurately, there has been another shift. As far as I can tell, the Yield sign has changed for me a few times. When I first started driving in the early eighties, it was a yellow diamond with black trim. As far as I can tell, in 2017, it was a red diamond with white trim and now it is a red upside-down triangle with white trim. And there seem to be many pictures of yellow triangle yield signs online. I have had several conversations with people about the red diamond

Yield sign. When people would question it, I would show them pictures of it on the internet. No one ever argued with me saying that it was a triangle and not a diamond. It is so hard for me now, to even picture the red diamond Yield sign. Why is that? I recall it, in my memory, so vividly because I spoke about it so much. But it's just gone. I cannot even find any residual.

I have also asked, "What weapon does the scarecrow carry, in the *Wizard of OZ*?" and "Is it, *Sex in the City* ~ or *Sex and the City?*" One recent question has been, "What does Dorothy Gale do to get back to Kansas?" And of course, the one question that drug me back into the Mandela Effect when I stated on a video that I was done chasing Mandela Effects, "How many people were in the car when J.F.K. was murdered?" The interviews themselves were fun and informative but hard to do while tending bar.

There was someone on YouTube claiming to notice a change in the name brand Anheuser-Busch. I have no idea one way or the other what the spelling would have been or should be. I do know that when I walked across the street that same day I noticed a painted advertisement on the wall that was painted in the early nineteen hundreds or earlier that has the brand name spelled *'Ainheuser'*, plain as day. Residue or distortions may come from others who shifted from a Timeline similar to the one you recall, in my opinion.

The idea for me is to spread the word and get the idea out of people's heads that it is just confabulation because when they Googled it, that is what it told them. Well, Google may be in on this, as it had to catch up with my searches several times. Once I was searching for the now infamous Captain Picard Crystal. A YouTube channel called *Hidden Knowledge*, mentioned that *Captain Jean-Luc Picard* carried a quartz crystal in his hand for about a third of the episodes.

Well, I knew this was impossible as I owned a Quartz crystal remarkably similar to the one, they were showing. I search it and I was surprised to see a single picture with Picard holding this quartz crystal. I was floored. Yet, with all of the experiences I have had it still surprises me when I see a Mandela Effect, I am one hundred percent sure of. I decided to do a video on the crystal and started doing some research. Right on my video I show that there is no crystal anywhere to be found. About an hour later, on another search engine I tried the same search and I see two maybe three pictures of the crystal. And the next day the two search engines were inundated with Placard crystals. You can even buy it as a prop.

I feel the truth is the most important thing, whatever the truth may be for you. My YouTube channel name is Susso which covers most of my experiences. Whatever I can do to spread the word, I feel moved to complete. But, for myself, even though I still get excited when witnessing a new one hundred percent Mandela Effect, I refuse to chase Mandela Effects. I feel I am beyond the Mandela Effects in that they are merely sign posts, which in turn reminds me to continue creating.

It pays to be cautious while exploring someone else's information and research. Including mine. I am no exception. I say this because my interpretations of events may be interpreted differently by you. And I am also only relaying the experiences that have happened to me. It may be that these experiences have not happened to you. You are just taking my word for it that these things have really happened to me. Well, they have, and I have not exaggerated one iota. So, take what you can use from it and leave the rest. Use that and stop giving your power away to the television, government and religion. Discern for yourself and take no one's answer as absolute.

FOCUS, FUTURE & CONCLUSIONS

There are many theories as to what the Mandela Effect is. And that is just it, they are all theories and hypothesis. Even my ideas are just theories. And yes, they are based on experience, but they are my experiences not anyone else's. Many of the theories and hypotheses are very well put together and some of them could be placed into other theories having multiple possibilities be true. But even with the experiences I have had, no matter how I interpret the experiences and no matter how sure I am of the theory that, we are multidimensional beings experiencing multiple timelines by shifting our consciousness through different adjacent reality timelines, the honest response is that, I just don't know. Even with the positive results I have been having with creating, no matter how small the miracle may seem, I just do not know, for sure. *What if I told you*, that one of the theories on why things are changing is that we are living in a computer program and we are being controlled by an artificial intelligence, like in the movie *'The Matrix'*. On a side note, the phrase *'What if I told you'*, has never been said in the Movie *'The Matrix'*, in this Timeline.

Although, the computer simulation theory is a plausible theory, I tend to lean away from this one. Why? Because if it is true and it is also true that there are infinite timelines, I do not have to experience that if I do not desire to. Are we stuck in a program? Is the artificial intelligence making me believe I am creating? Is it telling me through other people what I should believe and do? After all of the experiences with the paranormal, which is probably normal in one Timeline or another, if there is an A.I. at work, it is only part of the answer. I say this because the game would already be over. Nothing I did would matter, if my every move were being controlled. No, I feel I have control and that there is much more involved.

I have decided to create my reality by focusing on my intent and not what others think my intent should be. I will create the physical reality I wish to experience. I will do this by aligning my desire with my heart. I cannot align my desire with the thinking part of my mind, as it has been polluted over many years through television, movies, music and news, among a plethora of advertisements you don't even know you see every day. In truth I am still experimenting, and I am an infant in this possible constructed world of creation.

These terms and systematic process is by no means a complete design of how to shift your consciousness into a different reality, but it seems to be the basis for what I have been creating. After a year of experimenting with desire and intent and the recipe I have formulated to shift my consciousness, I am at a point where it is all becoming one. There will be no process or ritual to perform if I continue to practice this technique. So, why wouldn't I just keep on creating? Why do I let myself get wrapped up in the physical reality around me? Physical reality does tend to get in the way. Yet, being in my own way, would be the first thing to overcome.

The only thing in the way, is my focus. Because my focus is what I will experience. If I am not informed of a catastrophe and it is headed my way, I will deal with that when or if it occurs. If people are being killed and it is coming my way, I will deal with it when it occurs. If I die … wait? If I die? There is no fear of anything and that is how we all need to live our lives, whether you focus on living in a Timeline where at every turn the next disaster is about to take place or you choose to focus on a more peaceful and loving Timeline, there should not be fear. Nor should you be giving your power away to any other beings or persons. It is your power. Take it and run with it! Pray, Meditate or Decree if that is the vibration you are resonating. But to give away your power in fear sounds pitiful to me. When I leave this Realm, I will leave this realm. If God or the Creator wants something of me, it can have it without asking. It can take me without asking. I really have no say. When you worship something or someone, it is my understanding that you are doing nothing but begging and throwing your God given power away, even if you are giving it back to God. Is that what God had in mind? I suppose it is your choice if you choose to give your power away. I will not beg for my life, because it is not my life to beg for. It is His. So, why fear? There is nothing you can do about it. It will or will not happen. It is happening or it is not happening. It already happened or it will not happen at all.

As I mentioned, I was brought up Catholic. And as much as I try to turn my back on all religion, I would not be the person I am today if it weren't for this upbringing. This religion taught me to question things. Sure, I would get a wrap across the mouth when I would ask something like why can't women be priests? But it also made me ask the question, which religion was the right religion, which brought forth all kinds of other questions. So, when I bring up God or religion, it is truly not from anything I am an expert on, but I do have a background in religion and have studied other religions for comparison. My beliefs have changed a number of times and I am aware that beliefs are nothing more than beliefs. They are not truth. Yet, with all of this said, with the Mandela Effect events and Flat Earth information, we now know that facts, truths and beliefs change.

For me, I will create. I will create until I am forced not to or taken from this Realm or reverted back into a baby avatar. But I don't think those things actually happen. I think, I inspire, I desire, I focus, and I know that I will live in a Timeline or Dimension, where Human Beings fly without mechanics. That I will be able to experience more than one Timeline consciously and project my quantum physical body in more than one place at a time. I will focus my Dominate Consciousness to exist in a Timeline, Dimension, Density or Reality, where to flow through Time and experience Time however one wishes, is commonly known and widely accepted. What a wonderful diverse experience that is.

I invite each and every one of you to expand your consciousness. Believe and follow the idea that you can have whatever experience you desire. You do not have to accept what others tell you is coming or will happen. You do not have to focus on Armageddon. You can join those waiting for a spiritual and physical battle if you are so called. But what I feel we all need to do is feel with our hearts, so we can figure out what it is we all want to experience as a collective. Will you have to fight in a war whether spiritual or physical? Do you desire this experience? You may not have to or maybe that is where your vibration is taking you and that is just what you need. I am not here to tell you what you need, that, of course, is up to you. I feel we have already bypassed a few wars and catastrophes. At least for me, I have shifted away from those things, even if it took death. Create your own reality! Live the life you want to live! Do not listen to any man or government, just feel and listen to your heart. Consider doing the work for yourself. How will you ever learn if everything is done for you? Get up and do the things Jesus did and do greater things than he did, because he, as well as you, has gone to the father, in your heart. Know John 14:12 and understand that passage. Know and understand that what you feel in your heart, what you believe and what you focus on is what physical life you will experience. If you feel the need to follow others, a church or priest, if you feel the need to listen to others because you need to be informed, try listening to yourself, because you already have all the answers within you. Stop polluting your mind with the media garbage. Especially since that garbage is geared to make you give away your God given power, freely.

As I write this, I couldn't help but recall the past few months. Specifically, August and September of 2017 and the end of January of 2018. They were like the experiences I had while reading the Mandela Effect site memory threads back in 2015. There was some discomfort and I could feel negativity leaving my body. I was disoriented and the people around me were annoying. I did not know it was happening while it was occurring. I have also noticed that when many people seem to get the flu, many also notice new Mandela Effects. Could it be that some people are just getting used to their new physical body?

I feel we shift our consciousness through timelines often. I feel when understanding our energy and who we are in relation to our perspective we can manipulate and use this information to explore and shift to what we find more appealing. I think it is also very plausible that the Mass Forced Shifts occur at least twice a year. I have noticed this idea taking place each May and September. I do not believe these mass shifts are instant. I feel they take some time. But within ourselves, I feel we already have the ability to shift instantly, any time we want, to whatever Timeline we desire.

There are many views and ideas based on the Mandela Effects. I hope you explore them all and come up with some of your own theories. I hope you write about your own experiences and question. Yes, you will be attacked. Just remember, no one is wrong. They were just in a different timeline than you were when they experienced the event in question. Someday, the masses who listen to everything the media says, the people who swear there have been no changes to history, will not be able to deny it, even when the media comes up with a plausible explanation. The more people that write and vlog about this phenomenon, the bigger it will get and the stronger the momentum will be and one day, depending on where your focus is, you may witness the truth, more deception or you may experience Heaven on Earth. It's your choice.

I have interpreted my experiences and I understand that we are Multidimensional Beings Shifting our

Consciousness through Timelines to experience motion and time all the while creating the moment at hand. We are creating every moment right now and we always have been. We have just been manipulated to think and feel another way. We are not creating properly, as we tend to create with our minds rather than our hearts. That is how we have been programed to create, giving others all the power. Take their power away by not feeding the machine. Find creative things to do with your spare time instead of watching the news or playing a video game. Get out there and dig your feet into Mother Earth. If you are not sure how you look within yourself and you have no idea where to turn, get out into Nature and look at Mother Earth's beauty. She will respond to you because she is a living breathing being. And I feel that all who have been affected by this thing that has been labeled The Mandela Effect, are seeing these events because the veil has been lifted in some way. Use that and feel with your heart, discern what information you feed your mind and look and feel your way into a Timeline worth living in.

I feel that much of what we are experiencing these days is what we have already created. We may have been manipulated into creating certain outcomes, but we did it all the same. We let it happen. And now is the time for us to take our power back.

What you believe, or more accurately what you focus on is what you will experience. If you are focused on a theory about this Mandela Effect phenomenon, be it a computer program or a multiverse, religious experience or government program, then that is what you will experience as a means to an end. Your mind will create what it is you need to understand, and only show you what you can handle. I dislike using the term 'ascension', because of what the word has represented from new age teachings, but it is as good a word as any if used in the proper context. If we are ascending to a higher vibration of life, then this three-dimensional physical life will show you, through your beliefs, how or what you are supposed to do. I also feel and understand that this is important now, as soon, I feel three-dimensional reality is going to be stripped away.

I feel that if there is something bigger on its way; that it is wonderful yet may be very confusing for those that don't see, or are refusing to see, the Mandela Effects. I feel and focus on the love that I am going into. I focus on this new Earth that is spoken about. See, for me this new Earth is filled with infinite possibilities. Infinite timelines within the parameters of that specific new Earth and all of the timelines that are and will be unfolding there. It is already here. In my opinion, the Christ that is spoken about, is already here. That specific Christ energy is here and can be used by those who follow those teachings. But only if they truly believe it in their hearts. Do those who follow those teachings really believe the words spoken by the man known as Jesus? The man who brought the Christ Light into embodiment. Isn't that what he said we should thrive to do? Well, that is my intermediate interpretation, as there are others far more versed with such things.

If one is focused on these beliefs, or the teachings of any other religion, or no religion at all, it matters not. As long as they believe and follow their hearts, all will experience what they specifically need to experience individually to find their truth. Your heart is where you will find your answers. Your heart is where you will find your truth and if you so desire, it will guide you to shift the truth, to bend it and to mold it, into something more to your liking. My focus is that physical life is precious, and it is truly ours to live happily and freely. It is our birthright to experience physical life as malleable and ever changing.

In closing, I would like to add that I do in fact feel that there is something different, possibly something more extravagant on its way, which will wake and/or confuse those who have not seen things like the Mandela Effect. This something could be those who have not noticed changes, will now notice and those who have noticed will see something else altogether. I feel the most stubborn hearts will be opened. That being said also understand that those who do not notice Mandela Effects and the like, may not be ready to move on to something different. If this is in fact Quantum and Infinite, and we are all in our own Dimension, then those who do not see now, will see in their own time.

I think it is plausible that those who have seen identified Mandela Effects, will now see more Personal Mandela Effects, not being able to collaborate with others. I feel that for those who have seen incredible, wondrous things like the Mandela Effect, that it is their job to guide the unaware to an awakened state and let them choose their own path, as it can only be their choice. I also feel that it will be the job of those who have witnessed these miraculous things, to help those who will become fearful and confused, in the coming days. And if you feel the call to do something now, get out there on social media and preach what you have witnessed. Not just YouTube and Reddit, but as many different outlets as you can find. Tell people of the wonderous experiences you have had. Explain the Mandela Effect whichever way you are comfortable with. To those who have been affected by the Mandela Effect, get out there and write a book, write songs or poetry about your experiences.

And finally, as there are many plausible theories and hypotheses out there on what the Mandela Effect is and what is causing it, understand that whatever theory or hypothesis that resonates with your heart is the one you should lean towards. I am not saying believe anything, as we know now that beliefs can change. But, if there is something, anything that helps you cope with all of the lies you have been force fed throughout your entire life, then that is the theory or hypothesis you should focus on. We will fly!

This Is The Only Beginning ...

Proverbs 21:28
A false witness shall perish: but the man that heareth, speaketh constantly.

Job 14:14
If a man die, shall he live again? All the days of my appointed time will I wait, till my change come.

Acts 22:15
For thou shalt be his witness unto all men of what thou hast seen and heard.

1 Corinthians 15:51
Behold, I shew you a mystery; we shall not all sleep, but we shall all be changed ...

Titus 1:13
This witness is true. Wherefore rebuke them sharply, that they may be sound in the faith;

John 14:12
Verily, verily, I say unto you, He that believeth on me, the works that I do shall he do also; and greater works than these shall he do; because I go unto my Father.

There are great works being done on this subject, by some fantastic people. Many different theories, many different points of view. Here are just a few. Please, feel free to explore the following *YouTube Channels* for more research on the Mandela Effect & more …

Susso *(Author's YouTube Channel)*
Mind Beyond Matter *(Book Channel)*
photohelix *(Interview & Research Channel)*
scarabperformance *(Interview Channel)*
Brian Staveley *(Researcher & Reporter)*
DIRTH *(Flat Earth Researcher)*
jeranismRAW *(Reporter)*
The TruthSeeker69 *(Reset Investigator)*
The Dollar Vigilante *(Reporter)*
Shawn Indigo *(Reporter)*
NoblenessDee *(Investigator)*
Unbiased and on the Fence *(Support)*
chick *(Researcher)*
Armor Up! *(Support)*
Merkaba Carpet *(Guidance)*
Vannessa VA *(Researcher)*
Cynthia Sue Larson *(Quantum Jumping)*
Moneybags73 *(Mandela Effect Poll Channel)*